BUSINESS ECOSYSTEMS IN CHINA

We cannot afford to miss the remarkable rise of Chinese business ecosystems. Alibaba and their peers Baidu, Tencent, Xiaomi, and LeEco showcase unprecedented growth and success in China and are expanding their impact globally. With a combined market capitalization of close to 600 billion USD, incubating over 1,000 new ventures and an average annual growth of over 50%, they have become a force to reckon with for the likes of Google, Microsoft, Apple, Amazon, and IBM. 'Business ecosystem' is a frequently used concept to describe the unique competitive advantages of the American technology giants. This book explores not only the application of a business ecosystem approach in the Chinese context but also deals with the key strategic question: How did these five Chinese business ecosystems grow so rapidly and successfully?

The book takes the growth and transformation of Alibaba's business ecosystem as a focus case in comparison with Baidu, Tencent, Xiaomi, and LeEco. These business ecosystems developed in less than 20 years and transformed from organic growth to rapid expansion by investment and acquisition, entrepreneurship and incubation of new ventures, continuous innovation, and internationalization. This book brings insights and practical lessons on leading, creating, and disrupting markets for corporate executives and professionals in global business, a comparative case study for researchers and students of management, and food for thought on Chinese ways of doing business.

Mark J. Greeven is a Chinese-speaking Dutch Professor of Innovation and Entrepreneurship at Zhejiang University, China. For over a decade he has been collaborating with innovative Chinese companies and entrepreneurial multinationals. His work has been published in academic journals and newspapers like *The Financial Times* and *China Daily*. He is on the 2017 Thinkers50 Radar list of 30 next generation business gurus.

Wei Wei is an entrepreneur, investment professional, and the founder of GSL (www.gslpartner.com), an innovation management consultancy. Combining international experience in engineering and venture capital, she helps multinationals and ventures improve innovation practices and achieve growth. She received master degrees in engineering from Tsinghua University and RWTH Aachen University.

BUSINESS ECOSYSTEMS IN CHINA

Alibaba and Competing Baidu, Tencent, Xiaomi and LeEco

Mark J. Greeven and
Wei Wei

Routledge
Taylor & Francis Group

LONDON AND NEW YORK

First published 2018
by Routledge
2 Park Square, Milton Park, Abingdon, Oxon OX14 4RN

and by Routledge
711 Third Avenue, New York, NY 10017

Routledge is an imprint of the Taylor & Francis Group, an informa business

British Library Cataloguing in Publication Data
A catalogue record for this book is available from the British Library

Library of Congress Cataloging in Publication Data
Names: Greeven, Mark J., author. | Wei, Wei, 1984 April 5- author.
Title: Business ecosystems in China : Alibaba and competing Baidu, Tencent, Xiaomi and Leeco / by Mark J. Greeven and Wei Wei.
Description: Abingdon, Oxon; New York, NY: Routledge, 2018. |
Includes bibliographical references and index.
Identifiers: LCCN 2017014682| ISBN 9781138630949 (hardback) | ISBN 9781138630956 (pbk.) | ISBN 9781315209142 (ebook)
Subjects: LCSH: Information technology—Economic aspects—China. | New business enterprises—China. | Business incubators—China. | Electronic commerce—China.
Classification: LCC HC430.I55 G74 2018 | DDC 381/.14206551—dc23
LC record available at https://lccn.loc.gov/2017014682

ISBN: 978-1-138-63094-9 (hbk)
ISBN: 978-1-138-63095-6 (pbk)
ISBN: 978-1-315-20914-2 (ebk)

Typeset in Bembo Std
by diacriTech, Chennai

CONTENTS

FIGURES

TABLES

PREFACE

The initial interest in Alibaba came from the first author's field research at Zhejiang University, Hangzhou, China and meeting Alibaba founder Ma Yun in 2006. During the 2008 conference '*The Network Experience – New Value from Smart Business Networks*' in Beijing, the interest in investigating Alibaba from a business ecosystem perspective was sparked. During this conference the first author met Dr. Lu Liang, former R&D director of Taobao and former CEO of Huashu Taobao, and the second author at Tsinghua University. Subsequent research with Yang Shengyun and Yue Tao at the Rotterdam School of Management, Erasmus University and later the RSM Case Center has proven useful in developing the early ideas on business ecosystems. The output, several case studies on Alibaba in 2010 and 2016, allowed the authors to try out ideas and figure out key insights together with the many students that have used the cases. The thesis research work on knowledge sharing within Alibaba Group in 2013 by Frido van Driem is gratefully acknowledged.

While the initial work has been important, the real tough job was to create a reliable database on the investment activities of BATXL and understand the growth strategies. The authors gratefully acknowledge the work of our Zhejiang University research assistant Hou Shiyu. Moreover, our gratitude is to the School of Management, Zhejiang University for facilitating the research from 2011–2016. Nevertheless, inspiration and research have been only two of the fundaments of this book. Equally important has been the continuous verification, discussion and sometimes criticism from our Global Entrepreneurship MBA students (2012–2015) on various ideas and thoughts of business ecosystems, business models and digital disruption in China. The China Europe International Business School (CEIBS) Centre for China Innovation and their former co-directors George Yip and Bruce McKern have been kind enough to provide a platform in their Innovation Forums. Moreover, the participants of our workshops and corporate training programs with companies such as DSM, Bosch, Sanofi, Jones-Lange Lasalle, Philips, Honeywell and others have provided critical and reflective perspectives on our ideas and helped to develop the key insights from a business and professional perspective. Without the support and insights of our friends, former Alibaba employees, entrepreneurs such as Li Zhiguo and Lu Liang and other kind supporters of our journey, this book could not have been written.

Last but not least, both authors thank their families for the months of support, understanding and providing the perfect environment for writing in the summer and winter holidays of 2016–2017. A special thanks to Karen for proofreading and commenting on the manuscript. It must be noted that writing on such dynamic businesses as BATXL, change is the only constant. Although we have gone to great lengths to be up to date until the publication of our book, the future of BATXL is constantly changing. Therefore, we hope that the readers of this book will be inspired by their business ecosystem as an organizational form, which allows BATXL to constantly adapt and improve; innovation is the driver of these business ecosystems. While the above people have provided all the necessary support, the final responsibility lies with both authors and therefore any and all mistakes or errors remain with the authors.

Mark Greeven & Wei Wei

PART I
Business ecosystems in China

1

RISE OF BUSINESS ECOSYSTEMS IN CHINA

1.1 Introduction

At the end of the 1990s in China, three young men saw the rise of the Internet and started crafting business ideas. While one man was based in Beijing and was part of a bustling technology scene, the two other men were in the newly emerging Hangzhou (East coast) and Shenzhen (South coast). They independently built three Internet platforms in a time when most Chinese people had not heard of the Internet, and did not own computers, or credit cards for that matter. Within less than two decades these three platforms grew into China's largest business ecosystems encompassing online and offline businesses with a combined estimated market capitalization of over 500 billion USD by the end of 2016. These three men are Ma Yun, Li Yanhong and Ma Huateng and they respectively established Alibaba, Baidu and Tencent.

Ma Yun's business has its roots in trading and ecommerce, mostly focusing on facilitating small and medium enterprises in global market places. Li Yanhong's core business is search technology and is often dubbed the 'Google of China'. Ma Huateng's business has its roots in instant messaging and online communication. Nevertheless, all three platforms have been diversifying in the last five years into Internet finance, digital healthcare, culture and entertainment, enterprise services and location based services, among others. Moreover, they have incubated a combined total of over 1,000 new ventures. Transforming from three independent platforms to three competing business ecosystems, these three pioneers are now commonly known as BAT.

Then, in 2004 a small online video platform was established by a young man named Jia Yueting. It would be impossible for him to imagine that only ten years later he will openly and publicly challenge the mighty BAT and have an estimated market capitalization of 50 billion USD by the beginning of 2017. His video platform transformed into one the most innovative business ecosystems in China: LeEco.

The business ecosystem includes businesses ranging from entertainment production, smart TVs and smartphones to driverless cars; his ecosystem includes already four unicorns, i.e. a company with over 1 billion USD valuation before IPO. Although BAT is equally successful in their diversified investments, the new kid on the block posed a serious challenge.

However, as with everything in China, the story took a sudden turn when in 2010 several Chinese technology veterans established Xiaomi. With the speed of light and an unheard of business model that revolutionized online social marketing and built an instant fan base while lacking hardware R&D, production facilities and offline sales channels, Lei Jun and his co-founders were able to launch a smartphone that conquered the hearts of many young Chinese. It took only two years to surpass the Chinese market share of Apple and enter the national smartphone top five. After initial success, Lei Jun announced their five year plan and started building a Xiaomi family of hardware products, including TVs, air purifiers, smart wearables and rice cookers. They not only challenged local traditional manufacturers and BAT but also established multinationals as an underdog in their familiar markets.

What do these entrepreneurs and their success stories have in common? They strategically used business ecosystems for their rapid growth, transformation and success in China. This book is about the business ecosystems of Baidu, Alibaba, Tencent, Xiaomi and LeEco (BATXL).

1.2 What this book is about

This book is about how leading Chinese companies adopt a business ecosystem approach to not only lead but also create and disrupt the market. The unique competitive advantage of American companies like Google, Microsoft and Apple is often attributed to the business ecosystem approach to organizing their businesses (e.g. Moore, 1996; Adner, 2006; Iansiti and Levien, 2004). Recently the popular (Chinese) press explained the success of Chinese pioneers such as Alibaba and Xiaomi in a similar way. For instance, a search on Chinese search engine Baidu on the keyword 'business ecosystem' (in Chinese: 'shangyeshengtai') gave 2.1 million results in Chinese in January 2017. The purpose of our book is to adopt and explore the business ecosystem concept in the Chinese context by providing a definitive and systematic account of Alibaba's growth and transformation as a business ecosystem in comparison with other leading Chinese business ecosystems: Baidu, Tencent, Xiaomi and LeEco. The book is written for business professionals, executives, academics and students seeking deep insight into the success of Alibaba's business ecosystem in comparative context; academics and students seeking a deeper understanding of comparative business ecosystems in the Chinese context; business professionals and executives seeking insights in the leading business ecosystems in China; and researchers of strategy, business ecosystem and innovation in general.

A business ecosystem refers to particular arrangements between organizations that combine their own products and service offerings into a relatively coherent and customer centric offering (Adner, 2006). Moore (1996), one of the early thinkers on business ecosystems, took business ecosystems as new patterns of competition, rather than as a specific strategy. Moore sees a business ecosystem as an "economic community supported by a foundation of interacting organizations and individuals – the organisms of the business world" (Moore, 1996: 26). Iansiti and Levien (2004) conceptualize business ecosystems as networks of firms that collectively provide competitive advantages. They perceive ecosystems as loose networks of suppliers, distributors, outsourcing firms, makers of related products or services, technology providers and hosts of other organizations that affect and are affected by the creation and delivery of a company's own offerings. Iansiti and Levien take a stakeholder perspective, including in particular non-business stakeholders such as media and regulators. Weill and Woerner (2015) note that companies establish an ecosystem by creating relationships with other providers that offer complementary but sometimes also competing services.

In our book we refer to business ecosystems as new organizational forms where the businesses are interdependent through a variety of equity relationships combining product and service offerings into a customer centric offering. While the boundaries of a business ecosystem are fluent and dynamic, we take equity relationships as a criteria to be included in the business ecosystem. Therefore, we can distinguish business ecosystems from companies (full ownership and diversified businesses organized in business units), holdings (organizations connected by equity based relationship but no specific mutual interdependencies or necessary synergies beyond financial arrangements), and business networks (loosely connected groups of companies), as illustrated in Table 1.1.

While previous contributions by Moore (1996), Adner (2006, 2013), Iansiti and Levien (2004) and Weill and Woerner (2015) provide a solid academic and professional basis for the exploration of business ecosystems, they, first of all, are mostly limited to the US market context and entirely miss the rise of *Chinese business ecosystems*. China's business context has been particularly conducive to new organizational forms that explore and exploit the dynamics in the market: the rise of entrepreneurialism, digital disruption, middle class boom and regulatory uncertainty. These conditions will be explored in Section 1.5. Second, while previous studies

TABLE 1.1 Comparing business ecosystems to other organizational forms

	Business Ecosystem	*Company*	*Holding*	*Business Network*
Ownership structure	Equity sharing	Single ownership	Equity sharing	No equity sharing
Industry involved	Related and diverse	Single or limited	Unrelated and diverse	Single or limited
Decision-making mechanism	Orchestrated and interdependent	Centralized	Decentralized and independent	Limited coordination

address some *strategic questions,* they fail to systematically explore important strategic questions such as how does an ecosystem grow? What is the role of investment and acquisition in ecosystem development? To what extent does an ecosystem facilitate innovation? What are the challenges for strategy making? Does an ecosystem provide specific opportunities for entrepreneurship and incubation of new ventures? And to what extent can ecosystems as business models be internationalized? We adopt a framework of strategic growth to investigate such questions for leading Chinese business ecosystems. In particular we will focus on four growth approaches: innovation, investment, incubation and internationalization. Third, instead of discussing *business context* and companies as two independent units of analysis, we emphasize that business ecosystems are both part of and interdependent with the business context. Last, most of the previous publications are descriptive and insightful but fail to put insights into *comparative perspective.* We will take the growth and transformation of Alibaba's business ecosystem as a focus case to explore the above topics. We will compare the business ecosystem of *Alibaba* with other leading Chinese business ecosystems *Baidu, Tencent, Xiaomi* and *LeEco* to explore differences and similarities in order to gain a better understanding of the strategic aspects of business ecosystems in general and in the Chinese context in particular. In Figure 1.1 we visualize our contributions.

1.3 BATXL: Alibaba, Baidu, Tencent, Xiaomi and LeEco

The book is organized around a large case study of Alibaba's ecosystem (part 2) and comparison with other leading Chinese ecosystems: Baidu, Tencent, Xiaomi and LeEco (part 3). Table 1.2 summarizes the key facts of BATXL.

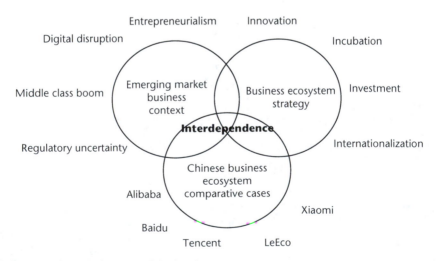

FIGURE 1.1 Contributions of this book

Source: authors' own figure.

TABLE 1.2 Case studies in this book: BATXL

	Baidu	*Alibaba*	*Tencent*	*Xiaomi*	*LeEco*
Business origin	Search	Ecommerce	Instant Message	Smartphone	Video platform
Core founder	Li Yanhong	Ma Yun	Ma Huateng	Lei Jun	Jia Yueting
Year of establishment	2000	1999	1998	2010	2004
Employees	40,000	34,000	25,000	8,000	15,000
Revenues (2015, billion USD)	9.9	12.3	15.8	12	2
Market cap (January 2017, billion USD)	58	220	230	45	11

Source: website and annual reports from BATXL

Many accounts of BATXL have been published in the last couple of years. We suggest readers interested in the more personalized or journalistic stories of the various companies and founders read the following books. Erisman (2015) is an insightful yet more journalistic account of Alibaba, providing insights based on the author's employment as head of international marketing until 2008. It provides an account on Alibaba's role as harbinger of new global business. Clark (2016) provides a more personal story of Ma Yun. It is filled with anecdotes and personal reminiscences but mostly emphasizes the positive aspects and Alibaba's local context. Lee and Song (2016) contains more than 200 quotes and aims to provide a direct look into the mind of Ma Yun. Many of these quotes are translated directly from the Chinese press and interviews. While the above books certainly document the development of Alibaba and describe Ma Yun's achievements, these accounts are of more journalistic nature with limited academic basis. Moreover, the books neither provide a comparative perspective nor explore strategic questions in Alibaba's ecosystem.

Baidu and founder Li Yanhong have been reported or described in over 50 Chinese book publications. Tencent and founder Ma Huateng have received significant attention in the Chinese press as well, noted in over 60 books, and a recent publication in English by Lin and Zhang (2013). Many of these publications are descriptive, focusing on Ma Huateng and his partners, friends and investors, describing the early growth of Tencent. An interesting exception may be Peng (2016), who describes the history and development of Tencent, its diversification strategy and partnership model. Xiaomi and founder Lei Jun have recently gotten more attention. Shirky (2015) focuses on the reasons of Xiaomi's rapid success and how it is connected to China's economic growth. Li (2016) discusses the early success of Xiaomi, viral marketing and social media brand building, as described by the co-founder of Xiaomi. It is noteworthy that there are over 75 books written in Chinese on Xiaomi. There are not many detailed publications on LeEco and founder Jia Yueting but a lot of news media reports.

Only a few books deal with more than one of the business ecosystems under investigation. For instance, Hu (2014) compares Alibaba and Tencent in his book. The focus of the book is on the increasing competition in Internet in China, mostly analysing the operations of both companies and their predictions of future trends. For readers interested in a summary of the development of Alibaba, Tencent and Xiaomi's early years, the book by Tse (2015) is recommended. It focuses on the importance of entrepreneurs in China's economy while highlighting the developments of selected cases.

1.4 Our research

Our research for this book has four major strands. The first strand of research is an extensive empirical research program that includes three phases of interviews with (former) Alibaba employees and entrepreneurs such as Li Zhiguo and Lu Liang in Alibaba's business ecosystem: a first round of interviews in 2007, a second round of interviews plus an internal survey in 2011, and a third round of interviews in 2016. The first part of the research program was carried while the first author was employed by the Rotterdam School of Management, Erasmus University, with the local facilitation of Zhejiang University in Hangzhou, where the first author has held a full time faculty position since 2011 and a visiting research position in 2007–2008. Parts of this research program have been transformed into a series of teaching cases jointly published by both authors in The Case Centre, a case study in the *Financial Times* and a chapter on Alibaba and Ma Yun (see: Greeven et al., 2016a, b; Greeven, 2014; Greeven et al., 2010, 2012).

The second strand of research is a comprehensive data collection effort by the authors on the investment and acquisition behaviour of the five ecosystems. In our research, we tracked and collected the number of deals, time, investment amount, amount of share acquired, investment type, investment domain, region of every investment and acquisition of BATXL. We also tracked whether or not the investments were made together with other investors. We collected this information from public English and Chinese sources including platforms that focus on investment (e.g. Zero2IPO, ITJuzi, China Venture), media that specialize in finance and business (e.g. *Financial Times, Forbes, Sina, Bloomberg)*, Alibaba's own media channels (e.g. Alizila) and news reports by BATXL. The database is originally built and owned by the authors. The BATXL database is unique and provides systematic and comprehensive data on BATXL's investment behaviour. Please note that our database includes the publicly available information or disclosed information by the five ecosystems. Of course, it is likely that they have had more investments that were either not disclosed or not with a visible product launched in the market. For instance, Lei Jun announced in December 2016 that they have invested in 77 projects, of which about 30 of them successfully launched products and disclosed information. Based on discussion with investment professionals and external verification, it is likely that the other ecosystems have a similar situation. Therefore, our database is consistent and representative for BATXL's investment strategy.

The third strand of research is the review of extant secondary material in English and Chinese academic, professional and popular media; including the publically disclosed (annual) reports, SEC filings, news channels and financial statements of BATXL. Considering the rapid developments in China, the data collection efforts combined extensive triangulation of sources from a large variety of outlets to ensure relevance and robustness. As a former Chinese investment professional, the second author has access to channels and expertise to find relevant information, including statistics and insights from the professional investment world in China; while the first author employed academic resources, databases and verification from the academic world. Therefore, the research that is underlying this book includes both professional and academic secondary material, in both English and in Chinese. In Chapters 2, 7 and 8 we will not refer specifically to the large body of publications for the general story and description but indicate specific up-to-date data sources for financial figures and performance related indicators. Most of the up-to-date and recent data sources are in Chinese language publications such as Caijing, Sina, Hexun and Sohu and Chinese research centres, such as the CECRC and CNNIC.

The fourth strand of research is the authors' extensive presentation and discussion of the underlying research with Chinese and international executives and innovation professionals. In particular, the authors have benefited greatly from discussions with peers in the China Europe International Business School (CEIBS) and Zhejiang University and the various forums and conferences organized around the topic of innovation in China. Our frequent discussions with executives and innovation professionals from Fortune 500 companies have helped us to reflect on our research findings and create face validity of our findings and insights.

1.5 Rise of business ecosystems in China

What explains the rise of business ecosystems in China over the last decade? We distinguish four important drivers of the rise of business ecosystems in China, as illustrated in Table 1.3.

TABLE 1.3 Economic drivers and business needs in China's market

Economic drivers	Business needs
• Entrepreneurialism and venture capital	• Need for speed
• Internet boom	• Variety of product demand
• Growth of segmented middle class	• Uncertainty of market and regulation
• Dynamic regulatory environment	• Impatient capital

1.5.1 Rise of the private sector and impatient venture capital

The private sector is the driving force of China's economy. The number of small and medium sized enterprises (SMEs) in China has an annual average growth of 7% over the last two decades (China Statistical Yearbook, 2016). Bold reforms under the ninth Five Year Plan (5YP) 1995–2000 led to a greatly expanded role of the private sector. The private sector has become not only the main generator of output (an estimated 70% of GDP according to the China Statistical Yearbook, 2016) and employment, and strongest growth engine, but also the most active sector for innovation in China. Entrepreneurs with ambition and an eye for exploiting market opportunities are driving the developments in the private sector, in particular the technology sector in China.

In the 2016 Global Entrepreneurship Monitor (GEM) survey, the TEA (Total Early-age Entrepreneurial Activity) of China (10.3) is similar to India (10.6), Israel (11.3) and the USA (12.6), and higher than the United Kingdom (8.8). From 2010 to 2014, the number of start-ups in China has doubled and reached 1,609,700, which was almost twice the amount of start-ups in the UK and India. The start-ups in China are booming especially in the high tech sector; while at the same time SMEs are increasingly embracing digital technology.

In 2015, China's government launched the 'Internet Plus' policy to encourage innovation and employ Internet and digital technology in traditional industries to achieve industry transformation and improve overall efficiency. The 'Mass Entrepreneurship and Innovation' policy was launched as a national strategy to encourage people to start their own businesses and to innovate their current business. While some initiatives are directed at mandating entrepreneurship education at institutions of higher education, other initiatives are more directed to support start-ups. In particular the increase in the number of start-up incubators in China is telling: the total number of incubators has tripled to over 1,500 in the last decade and by now one third are national level incubators, i.e. receiving national government support and subsidy.

Private risk capital has also seen an immense increase over the last decade, both in terms of number of deals and in total investment value. This ranges from angel investment to venture capital (VC) and private equity (PE) investment. Although the boundaries of these types of investments have been blurry for most of the time in China, we see in recent years a growing number of investors focusing on the early stage companies and the affluent class is also embracing angel investment. According to Zero2IPO (2015) the volume of venture capital investment rose from 1.7 billion USD in 2004 to over 17 billion USD in 2015. The amount of deals increased twelvefold from 250 deals in 2004 to 3,100 deals in 2015. Moreover, since 2015 we see a strong influx of USD funds as compared to RMB funds investing in the market.

In 2015 China's VC environment was thriving and promising with over 3,000 investors injecting over 17 billion USD in the market. Although there was a downturn in 2012 and 2013, especially due to the limited exit options once domestic IPOs were prohibited for over a year, the momentum picked up drastically in 2014 thanks to the booming of the Internet industry. In 2015 the Internet industry absorbed 31% of all

VC investments. Nevertheless, comparing with markets like the USA, China's VC environment is still immature and relatively unprofessional, according to a PEStreet (2015) report. The scale of private investment (PE and VC) in the US was ten times that of China at the end of 2014. Pension funds are the largest player in the US PE market accounting for 25.3% of the capital, while private capital accounted for 13.9% in 2014. In China's PE market, however, the main player was private capital, and not until 2008 social insurance funds were allowed into the PE market with certain constraints. Moreover, there were only limited exit options, i.e. pay out, for PEs in China and IPO was the main method. China's PE market lacked professional investors and investing organizations. Most of them followed market trends to invest instead of relying on knowledge and experiences to independently judge the value of a company. Professional investors and observers would often refer to a VC boom in China, where second rate start-ups would relatively easily receive venture capital investments. While overall flow of private capital to start-ups is good, it may have the side effect of 'spoiling the market' and leaving less funds available for the better start-ups.

All in all, with the growing of the support from government, boom of start-ups, and rise of incubators as well as risk capital, the entrepreneurship ecosystem in China is maturing and companies create advantages by tapping into such ecosystems.

1.5.2 Internet boom

By the end of 2016, China had over 720 million Internet users, up from just 22 million in 2000; one fifth of the total world population online was now Chinese. Although these numbers and growth are remarkable, China had only reached a penetration rate of just over 50%, on the global average, but less than USA's 88%, according to Internet Live Stats (see Figure 1.2). The sheer size of

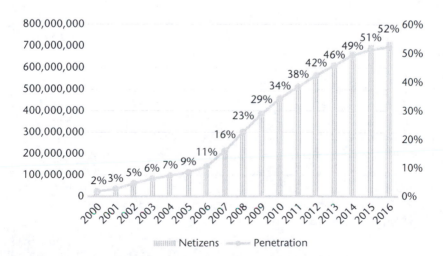

FIGURE 1.2 Netizens and internet penetration in China

Source: Internet Live Stats, 2017.

the online population has opened up many possibilities for online business but also for traditional business extending channels and combining online and offline business operations. The most recent trend is full connectivity where mobile Internet, manufacturing, marketing data and sales channels are increasingly being integrated.

The Internet economy is becoming one of the top industries in China, larger than traditional industries such as real estate, education and logistics. China's online trading volume has surpassed 30 trillion RMB in 2016 and is now the largest B2C and C2C ecommerce market in the world. The online retail market amounted to 3.88 trillion RMB with a year-on-year increase of 33% and occupied 11% of national consumer goods retail sales in 2015. Around 67.9% of Chinese consumers have bought clothes and accessories online and 53.6% have bought electrical appliances. There are many strong players in the ecommerce market, such as JD.com, VIP.com and Suning.com, but Taobao is dominant in the C2C market with more than 90% market share while Tmall occupies nearly 60% of the B2C market share in China (CECRC, 2016).

All in all, the Internet boom and associated opportunities make a unique time frame for new business driven by digital technologies and traditional business transformed by digital technologies. At the same time, the speed of the digital opportunity is so quick that even Internet driven companies need to compete at breakneck velocity. A business ecosystem approach facilitates such speed and allows experimentation with new business models.

1.5.3 Growth of a segmented middle class

China is seeing the largest consumption upgrade in the world. The predictions in McKinsey (2016) are that the percentage of households earning between 16,000 USD and 34,000 USD will increase from 6% in 2010 to over 50% in 2020. Consumer expenditure is expected to grow from 2,800 USD in 2014 to 4,500 USD in 2018. China's level of consumer spending still remains far below the USA's, but it is growing much faster, with a predicted annual average growth of 8%. We can speak of a true explosion of the middle class in China, boosting discretionary expenditures over the next years. In particular the upper middle class is likely to become the main engine of consumer spending over the next decade, while the USA has seen a sharp drop in the size of its middle class. The growth of the consumer market affects all sectors and in particular retail. Strong growth in the size and diversity of China's middle class will create new market opportunities for both domestic and international companies. In all, the strong growth of consumer demand is creating a positive push to the demand for higher quality, more and diverse products and services.

China's middle class, however, is fragmented and consists of different generations. As the Accenture Global Consumer Pulse Research shows in their annual consumer behaviour studies, Chinese consumers have become more sophisticated and care about service and experience of buying products, diversity, speed, reliability and quality. Ecommerce is tapping into those needs by fulfilling the long tail requirements, in particular providing a large diversity of choice, all across China, and providing convenience of transaction and delivery. The generation born in the mid to late 1980s and 1990s are the main consumption force. They grew up when China's economy was thriving and most of them were only children. Their parents had gone through hardships and often have a conservative consuming attitude. But their children like to try innovative things, care more about quality and identity, have higher brand loyalty, favour niche brands, and are used to Internet shopping. It is predicted that in ten years (2012–2022) the volume of consumption by this generation will double (Barton et al., 2013).

All in all, the growth of the segmented middle class provides a great opportunity for Chinese companies. At the same time, the diversity of demand and dynamics of the consumers requires companies to be more flexible and responsive. A business ecosystem approach facilitates such flexibility and responsiveness.

1.5.4 Dynamic regulatory environment

China has changed within four decades from a centrally planned socialist economy to a market oriented economy since the opening up and reform started in 1978. The current economy is characterized by a co-existence of socialist institutions and newly created, market based institutions. The legacy of state socialism is still largely ingrained and pervasive in current institutions and organizations, resulting in unexpected policy changes and unclear implications of policies. While China scores particularly low on governance indicators such as voice and accountability and protection of intellectual property rights, government effectiveness is continuously improving (World Bank, 2015). In the Global Entrepreneurship Monitor China scores high on internal market dynamics, global top 3. While market dynamics fuel entrepreneurship, too much dynamics also fuels uncertainty. The survey in the Global Entrepreneurship Monitor China indicates that over 40% of the investigated entrepreneurs show a fear of failure.

Sometimes the policy environment is supportive, as in the case of the recent promotion of innovation and entrepreneurship. From May 2013 to December 2015 there were at least 22 governmental documents released to promote innovation and entrepreneurship. Specifically in the field of Internet and online finance, after years of experimentation, the Chinese government has issued a range of guidelines and national strategies in 2014 and 2015 (see Table 1.4). Meanwhile China's business landscape is also characterized by sudden bursts of strong and strict regulation. A recent example is the regulation and control of the online taxi hailing market. Ride hailing has not been officially regulated in the past years but regulation was suddenly announced in November 2016. New controlling regulations on drivers and cars in cities like Shanghai, Beijing and Shenzhen will force the Chinese taxi hailing giant Didi Chuxing to standardize and operate more like a traditional taxi company.

TABLE 1.4 Selected recent policies of the Internet industry

Time	Abstract of the Policy
18 July 2015	The People's Bank of China issued guidelines for Internet financial sector.
24 Jun 2015	The State Council approved the guidelines on 'Internet plus' action plan.
20 Jun 2015	The State Council released a document to promote the development overseas ecommerce.
7 May 2015	The State Council released a document to support the development of ecommerce.
6 May 2015	Prime Minister Li Keqiang stated to initiate the 'Internet Plus' action plan in order to promote the development of Cloud calculation, ecommerce and Internet finance.
19 Mar 2015	The People's Bank of China released guidelines on mobile payment business.

All in all, China's dynamic regulatory environment which includes both positive and negative effects, at least requires companies to be agile, responsive and adaptable. While on the one hand, there is a strong domestic market demand, on the other hand, regulation is posing challenges or sudden opportunities. In such a market context, companies require speed and flexibility to survive and compete. A business ecosystem approach facilitates such flexibility and speed.

1.6 Reading guide

The book is organized around a large case study of Alibaba's business ecosystem. Chapter 2 discusses the transformation and *growth* of the ecosystem. Chapter 3 deals with how Alibaba has sped up the growth of its ecosystem by *investment* since 2013. Then, Chapter 4 discusses what happens inside Alibaba's ecosystem, with a particular focus on entrepreneurship and *incubation* of new ventures. Chapter 5 discusses how Alibaba has pioneered Internet finance in China, as an illustration of its continuous *innovation*. Lastly, Chapter 6 looks ahead and explores the *internationalization* of Alibaba's ecosystem. Then in the last part of the book we discuss (Chapters 7 and 8) and compare (Chapter 9) the four competing business ecosystems: Baidu, Tencent, Xiaomi and LeEco. Chapter 10 concludes and provides a discussion.

For those readers specifically interested in the transformation of Baidu, Alibaba, Tencent, Xiaomi and LeEco, Chapters 2, 7 and 8 are recommended. For those readers interested in a deeper understanding in Alibaba's growth strategies, we recommend Chapters 3–6. For the readers interested in how the business ecosystems of BATXL are diverging, we refer to Chapter 9. Those readers interested in the potential of internationalizing business ecosystems we refer to Chapter 6 (Alibaba) and Chapter 9 (comparison with Baidu, Tencent, Xiaomi and LeEco).

Notes for the reader:

- Use of Chinese names: we use the Chinese pinyin description of Chinese names where we put the family name first and given names second, i.e. Ma Huateng. Moreover, while many Chinese people have English names, we will only use their full Chinese names;
- Currency: we predominantly use the local currency RMB instead of conversions to USD. We intend to stay as close as possible to the original data and also note that last year's fluctuation of the USD-RMB exchange rate has been significant. As a rough guideline we recommend: 1 USD ~ 7 RMB;
- Chinese language: we will not use Chinese characters in this book when referring to specific Chinese terms but rather employ the Chinese pinyin system.

References

Adner, R., 2006. 'Match your innovation strategy to your innovation ecosystem', *Harvard Business Review*, 84(4), pp. 98–107.

Adner, R., 2013. *The wide lens: What successful innovators see that others miss*, New York, Portfolio/Penguin.

Barton, D., Chen, Y. and jin, A. 2013. Mapping China's middle class. *McKinsey Quarterly*, [online] Available at: http://www.mckinsey.com/industries/retail/our-insights/mapping-chinas-middle-class. Accessed 22/02/2017

CECRC, 2016. 2015 Nian du zhong guo dian zi shang wu shi chang shu ju [2015 China ecommerce market data]. *China Electronic Commerce Research Centre*. Available at: http://b2b.toocle.com/zt/2015ndbg/. Accessed 30/03/2016 [in Chinese]

China Statistical Yearbook, 2016. *National Bureau of Statistics of China*. Available at: http://www.stats.gov.cn/tjsj/ndsj/2016/indexeh.htm. Accessed 11/02/2017

Clark, D., 2016. *Alibaba: The house that Jack Ma built*, New York, Ecco.

Erisman, P., 2015. *Alibaba's world: How a remarkable Chinese company is changing the face of global business*, New York, St. Martin's Press.

Global Entrepreneurship Monitor, 2016. *Global Report*, [pdf] Global Entrepreneurship Research Association (GERA). Available at: http://www.gemconsortium.org/report/49812. Accessed 22/02/2017

Greeven, M.J., Yue, T., Wei, W., Koene, B. and Hou, S., 2016a. 'Alibaba's growth frenzy: Expanding by acquiring', *The Case Centre*, Reference no. 316-0195-1. Available at: http://www.thecasecentre.org/educators/products/view?id=136214. Accessed 11/02/2017.

Greeven, M.J., Yue, T., Wei, W., Koene, B. and Hou, S., 2016b. 'Alibaba's growth frenzy: Pioneer in China's Internet financial service', *The Case Centre*, reference no. 116-0065-1. Available at: http://www.thecasecentre.org/educators/products/view?id=136214. Accessed 11/ 02/2017.

Greeven, M.J., 2014. 'Alibaba group and Jack Ma', In F.L. Yu and H.D. Yan, ed. *Handbook in East Asia Entrepreneurship*, Chap. 33. London, Routledge.

Greeven, M.J., Yang, S.Y., Yue, T., Van Heck, E. and Krug, B., 2012. 'How Taobao bested eBay in China', *Financial Times*, 12 March.

Greeven, M.J., Yang, S., Heck, E. and Krug, B., 2010. 'The ecosystem of the Alibaba Group: How is Alibaba Group's strategy and implementation in China creating sustainable value for suppliers, partners and customers?', *The Case Centre*, Reference no. 310-125-1-2.

Hu, J.Z., 2014. *Yi dong hu lian wang zhi dian: Teng xun vs a li ba ba* [The peak of mobile Internet: Tencent vs. Alibaba], Beijing, People's Posts & Telecom Press [in Chinese].

Iansiti, M. and Levien, R., 2004 'Strategy as ecology', *Harvard Business Review*, 82 (3), pp. 68–78.

Internet Live Stats, 2016. Internet users by country, *Internet Live Stats*. Available at: http://www.lnternetlivestats.com/lnternet-users-by-country/. Accessed 22/02/2017

Lee, S. and Song, B., 2016 *Never give up: Jack Ma in his own words (In their own words)*, Evanston, IL, Agate B2.

Li, W.Q., 2016. *The Xiaomi way: Customer engagement strategies that built one of the largest smartphone companies in the world*, Columbus, OH, McGraw Hill Education.

Lin, J. and Zhang, Y.Z., 2013. *Ma hua teng de teng xun di guo* [The Tencent Empire of Ma Huateng], Beijing, China, Intercontinental Press [in Chinese]

McKinsey, 2016 *The modernization of the Chinese consumer*, [pdf] McKinsey. Available at: http://www.mckinseychina.com/wp-content/uploads/2016/03/The-Modernization-of-the-Chines e-Consumer_EN.pdf. Accessed 22/02/2017

Moore, J.F., 1996. *The death of competition: Leadership and strategy in the age of business ecosystems*, New York, HarperBusiness.

Peng, Y., 2016. *Teng xun di guo zhen xiang* [Tencent truth mosaic], Beijing, China: Electronics Press [in Chinese].

PEStreet, 2015. Zhong guo yu mei guo si mu ji jin shu ju bi jiao [Comparison of private equity fund data between China and the US]. Available at: http://www.pestreet.cn/article/2015000000058943.html. Accessed 22/02/2017 [in Chinese]

Shirky, C., 2015. *Little rice: Smartphones, Xiaomi, and the Chinese dream*, New York, Columbia Global Reports.

Tse, E., 2015. *China's disruptors: How Alibaba, Xiaomi, Tencent, and other companies are changing the rules of business*, London, Penguin.

Weill, P. and Woerner, S.L., 2015. 'Thriving in an increasingly digital ecosystem', *MIT Sloan Management Review*, 56 (4), pp. 27–34.

World Bank, 2015. *Worldwide governance indicators*, The World Bank Group. Available at: http://data.worldbank.org/data-catalog/worldwide-governance-indicators. Accessed 22/02/2017

Zero2IPO, 2015. 2015 Qian 11 yue VC tou zi chuang li shi xin gao, zhong tou zi e chao qian yi ren min bi' [November 2015 VC investment record of over 100 billion RMB]. Available at: http://research.pedaily.cn/201512/20151215391385.shtml. Accessed 22/02/2017 [in Chinese].

PART II
Alibaba case

2

ALIBABA'S ECOSYSTEM TRANSFORMATION

Strategic change

2.1 Introduction

Few companies transform themselves unless being forced by financial difficulties or business context changes. Nevertheless, it appears critical for companies to renew their capabilities rather than relying on historic capabilities. While business transformation is thus often forced by internal financial difficulties or external contextual forces such as regulation, technology and markets, Alibaba has been continuously transforming their business ecosystem, not just a response to internal or external forces. In this chapter we discuss the continuous transformation of Alibaba's ecosystem. The chapter draws on new research (see Section 1.4 for details) and previous research of the authors, Greeven (2014), Greeven et al. (2010, 2012), journalistic accounts by Clark (2016) and Erisman (2015) and the websites and annual reports of Alibaba Group (2016) and Alibaba's news portal Alizila.

2.2 Origin of Alibaba Group: Ma Yun

Ma Yun is from Hangzhou, the capital city of Zhejiang Province. He grew up during the Cultural Revolution and at an early age became interested in learning English. Since he was 12 he went to a hotel near the West Lake every morning to give free tours to foreign tourists to improve his English. He attended the Hangzhou Teacher's Institute (upgraded to Hangzhou Normal University in 1984) and graduated in 1988 with a bachelor's degree in English. He became an English teacher in the Hangzhou Dianzi University and established his first company, Hangzhou Hope Translation Agency (1994), and not long afterwards he tried his hand at China's first website (1995): China Business Page.

Ma Yun had limited knowledge of the Internet at that time. One of the first times he used a computer and the Internet was on a trip to the US. There he tried to search for 'China' and did not get many search results. Upon return he started the China Business Page. The website had a similar vision as the later Alibaba.com, to list Chinese companies on the Internet and make foreigners find Chinese websites. At the early phase of China Business Page, he tried to convince Chinese companies to post their business information on the website abroad and he charged for the advertisement fee. He would send a photo and 2,000 words of information of the company to the US by UPS and a US partner company would help him post the information online and then print the website page and send them back by UPS. China Business Page is the first Chinese business website. Most Chinese companies had never heard of websites; few companies would believe a product and service they had never seen. Ma Yun was not trusted for quite a long time until the website slowly gained popularity in China. Observers contend that because of the experience that Ma Yun was distrusted by others, he paid more attention to how people create trust and he knew more about how to make people trust each other.

In 1998 Ma Yun took up the job as general manager at an information technology company established by the China International Electronic Commerce Centre, a department of the Ministry of Foreign Trade and Economic Cooperation. He never got rid of the idea of setting up a company to achieve his vision and a year later he established Alibaba.com.

2.3 Beginning of an ecosystem

Launched in 1999, *Alibaba.com* is the flagship of the Alibaba Group, a global leading English language wholesale marketplace for global trade. Buyers are located in over 200 countries and include agents, wholesalers, SMEs, retailers and manufacturers. By 2017 the platform includes two distinct businesses: Alibaba .com International and 1688.com (formerly Alibaba.com China). Alibaba.com International is the leading global ecommerce platform for small businesses around the world. 1688.com is the leading domestic ecommerce platform for Chinese small businesses. Key in the development of Alibaba.com was the introduction of a fee-paying membership package that gave priority placement to stores and products. Furthermore, in collaboration with leading credit service companies Alibaba.com provides TrustPass profiles to reliable partners. TrustPass is a certificate issued by Asian Company Profiles (ACP), a third party credit agency. With the exclusive focus on SMEs and a combination of immediately monetizing the user base and selective early international expansion (such as Japan and India), Alibaba .com quickly became a premier brand in ecommerce.

In May 2003, Alibaba launched *Taobao*. Taobao offers a comprehensive range of products from collectibles and hard-to-find items to consumer electronics, clothing and accessories, sporting goods and household products. In less than ten years Taobao became one of the world's most popular consumer to consumer (C2C) ecommerce marketplaces. In 2008, the Group announced a further investment of RMB 50 billion in Taobao for the next five year period to upgrade the software and hardware systems and construct 'Taobao City', a high tech park West to Hangzhou, where Taobao would have its own Internet data centres. Ma Yun founded Taobao .com also as a defensive move to protect the Group from eBay's entry into China. When eBay launched in China it had global revenues of more than 2 billion USD. As a young, domestic entity, Taobao was taking on a huge rival while also fending off many similar small competitors in the ecommerce sector, where the barriers to entry were low. Taobao's key success factors include the choice of free listings, changing the apparent weakness of being a small Chinese company into strength (for instance, emphasizing Chinese culture by using Kong Fu names for moderators) and developing an innovative customer service in which customers can have instant communication with sellers via instant messenger Aliwangwang (Greeven et al., 2012). Moreover, trust has been crucial for the business transactions, as Ma Yun is aware of. The shop assessment and review system and instant communication in combination with strict reviewing and policy for new shopkeepers aims to safeguard trust and authenticity of the sellers.

Taobao.com took up the opportunity to become an online shopping landmark in China with an extensive brand selection and launched *Tmall* in April 2008. Tmall aims to be the online platform for quality, brand name goods serving the needs of increasingly sophisticated Chinese consumers. In June 2011, it was separated from Taobao's C2C marketplace and became an independent business to consumer (B2C) marketplace. It offers several digital malls, such as a consumer electronics mall, a book mall, a beauty mall and so on. Brands with flagship retail storefronts on Tmall.com include UNIQLO, L'Oreal, Adidas, P&G, Unilever and Levi's. Concluding, the core of Alibaba was built up and includes B2B, B2C and C2C platforms, which unite millions of buyers and suppliers and form the core of Alibaba's business ecosystem, as illustrated in Figure 2.1.

2.4 A decade of building an ecommerce ecosystem

In 2004 Alibaba's ecosystem sees its first large scale transformation. In the following decade the business ecosystem is maturing and all the services are extended to support the core to create a fully functioning ecommerce ecosystem. In particular we distinguish three phases: 1) extending SME client services; 2) extending consumer services; 3) consolidating and upgrading. In the latter

FIGURE 2.1   Alibaba ecosystem: core

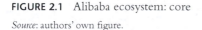
Source: authors' own figure.

phase we in particular notice the upgrading of the logistics from dependence on external providers to initiating a smart logistics network (Cainiao) and extending from Alipay's online payment to a fully fledged online financial services sub-ecosystem.

2.4.1 Phase 1: Extending SME client services

Alipay is introduced in 2004 shortly after the founding of Taobao. It is China's leading third party online payment platform, with a market share of 50% for over a decade. In 2008, it facilitated nearly 20 billion USD in online payment volume and had 48 million users, compared to 33 million credit card holders in China. Unlike other services, Alipay takes payments from the buyer directly and puts it in an escrow account, and later transfers the payment to the seller after the deal is completed, thereby creating the necessary safeguard that Chinese buyers and sellers need. Sellers can then be sure that payments will be honoured while buyers can be sure about commodity delivery and promises made by the sellers. As a first mover in the online payment market, it currently has partnerships with 170 financial institutions in China and abroad (including 14 foreign currencies). Alipay has been instrumental for the success of Taobao, not only differentiating it from its competitors but revolutionizing the payment market in China (Greeven et al., 2012).

However, Alipay is only one of the two legs that supports the expansion of Alibaba. The other leg is the quick rise of the local express delivery industry. In fact, the Chinese ecommerce and service delivery growth go hand in hand. After the development for the past decade, the top six express delivery companies, i.e. the state owned EMS and the private SF Express, STO Express, YTO Express, ZTO Express and Yunda Express, gained about 66% market share in China by the end of 2016. No doubt, they were all driven by orders from ecommerce platforms such as Alibaba. Acknowledging the importance of express delivery and efficient logistics, Alibaba would later co-found a smart logistics initiative.

Alibaba.com always focused on serving the needs of its clients, SMEs, and realized that many of the small online stores were growing larger. Since online shops also need online advertising and marketing strategies, Alibaba Group developed *Alimama* in 2007, initially independent from the Group, to become China's leading Internet advertising company with close to half a million media publishers as partners. Alimama.com was integrated into Alibaba's business ecosystem in October 2008. Moreover, to support the business processes of online shops in 2007, Alisoft was founded and the main product developed at that time was Aliwangwang. Aliwangwang is the instant messenger used on the ecommerce platforms such as Tmall and Taobao to facilitate direct communication between buyer and seller. However, the last news on Alisoft was in 2008 and afterwards there appears to be no more activity. It is likely, according to observers, that the initiatives moved in a newly developed software cloud.

In 2009 the Group was focusing on development of IT services and support infrastructure. *Alibaba Cloud* was founded to serve as a developer of platforms for cloud computing and big data management. Alibaba Cloud provides the necessary data and infrastructure support to the growth of Alibaba Group and the whole ecommerce ecosystem. It provides a comprehensive suite of Internet based computing services, including ecommerce data mining, high speed massive ecommerce data processing, and data customization. By 2017 Alibaba Cloud has become China's largest public cloud service and an international competitor for Amazon Web Services and Microsoft's Azure, even winning an international cloud computing competition in 2016 (see Section 6.5). Alibaba Cloud, as well as the other SME client services mentioned above, are all crucial parts of the Big Taobao strategy which was initiated in 2008 and aims to make Alibaba a provider of ecommerce infrastructure services for all ecommerce market participants. Figure 2.2 illustrates phase 1 of the second layer (extending SME client services).

2.4.2 Phase 2: Expanding consumer services

In 2010 and 2011, Alibaba Group extended its consumer services considerably. Reaching out to international markets, the Group built a global ecommerce marketplace made up of small business sellers in 2010: *AliExpress*. It offers a wide variety of consumer products in 40 major categories. At the moment it lists over 50 million products and has buyers in more than 200 countries. In March 2011 *Juhuasuan* was launched as a group buying platform, reaching a gross merchandise volume of 3 billion USD in 2012. Taobao's first *offline mall* appeared in Beijing in May 2011: Taobao Mall iFengChao Furniture Showroom. In October of the same year, the Group opened shopping search engine *eTao*, which provides information about products, sellers and discounts across the various Alibaba Group platforms, including group buying. In 2011, this platform became independent and aimed to help Chinese consumers making online purchase decisions. Initially, the search results included, among others, Taobao, Tmall, Amazon China, Dangdang, Gome

FIGURE 2.2 Alibaba ecosystem: second layer phase 1 (extending SME client services)
Source: author's own figure.

FIGURE 2.3 Alibaba ecosystem: second layer phase 2 (expanding consumer services)

Source: author's own figure.

and Yihaodian. However, by 2017, eTao has returned to their original business model. Figure 2.3 illustrates phase 2 of the second layer (expanding consumer services).

2.4.3 Phase 3: Consolidating and upgrading

In October 2014, Alibaba established *Ant Financial*, the former Ali Xiaowei Finance Service Group, a comprehensive financial services company positioning itself as inclusive finance to serve individuals and SMEs. Ma Yun and roughly 25 of the co-founders or early employees of Alibaba hold 76% of Ant Financial's shares. As reported, National Council for Social Security Fund held 5% of Ant Financial Group's share, while China Development Bank Capital and Postal Savings Bank of China held 3% respectively. Currently, Alibaba does not directly own shares of Ant Financial, only indirectly via their co-founders' ownership. However, as a result of a legal dispute with Alipay in 2011, Alibaba has the right to get 37.5% of the market cap value of Ant Financial after IPO paid out. Therefore, Alibaba has indirect ownership rights on the future earnings.

Within Ant Financial, Huabei is an online consumer loan for individuals to stimulate users to consume more on Taobao and Tmall, thus increasing the profit in Alibaba's ecommerce business. Ant Fortune together with Zhaocaibao and Yu'ebao provide wealth management services, utilizing Alibaba's extant channels and turning them into profit earning businesses. Zhima Credit is a credit system that generates historical and dynamic data from Alibaba and provides users' credit information to build trust in transactions. With increasing credit information, it boosts Alibaba related business and increases its revenue in ecommerce and financial business. In February 2017 Alibaba opened up the SME credit platform to the public. Ant Financial has become a sub ecosystem in its own right and Chapter 5 will discuss in detail the various financial innovations initiated by Ant Financial.

In 2013, the turnover of Taobao and Tmall, two major brands of Alibaba group, reached more than 248 billion USD, delivering 6 billion pieces by

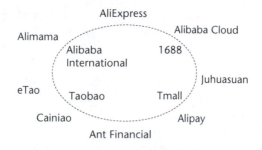

FIGURE 2.4   Alibaba ecosystem: second layer phase 3 (consolidating and upgrading)

Source: author's own figure.

Alibaba, producing more than 16 million parcels daily on average, 65% of the national express amount. In the same year, Alibaba co-founded *Cainiao* with several other companies, including the five major express delivery service providers. With the total investment of 300 billion RMB, Cainiao's goal is to create an intelligent backbone out of the current logistics chaos, to provide a services platform for ecommerce companies, logistics companies, warehousing companies and third party logistics service providers, and eventually realize 24 hour delivery nationwide.

Cainiao's ecosystem now includes delivery, warehousing, distribution centres, cross border delivery and courier services for rural areas; aiming to become a veritable ecosystem. The sub-ecosystem now claims to have 150 warehouses and 180,000 express delivery stations in China. By 2016, the service has covered 224 countries and regions, 2,800 counties in China. Through partnerships with couriers and warehouse service providers, the platform handles more than 70% of the parcels in China, boasting over 1.7 million delivery staff on the platform. Cainiao has become a closely knit network of stakeholders in logistics and we will discuss what happens in this ecosystem in more detail in Section 4.2. Figure 2.4 illustrates phase 3 of the second layer (consolidating and upgrading).

2.5 Diversification and creating new nodes

In 2013 Alibaba's ecosystem sees its second large scale transformation. Since then Alibaba has diversified from ecommerce to Internet related business, financial services, social networking services, digital healthcare, and culture and entertainment. The year 2013 marked Alibaba's investment strategy entering a new staging with larger amount investments in less mature companies and more diverse fields. In this latest development of Alibaba's business ecosystem we see the strategy of creating *new nodes* in the ecosystem, around which new sub-ecosystems develop. It is important to note that the new nodes do not necessarily support or facilitate the core ecommerce business. Moreover, many of the new nodes are experiments rather than necessary functions and businesses. In a way the business ecosystem is diversifying to satisfy non-current needs in the ecosystem.

Not content with just running online shopping marketplaces, Alibaba had built an ecommerce ecosystem to enable and support an expanding range of commercial activities. The goal was to make the Internet part of the Chinese consumer's everyday shopping experience: mobile apps like Alipay and Taobao let users pay electronically in physical shops, order movie tickets and take-out noodles, book transportation, and buy merchandise online but pick their orders up at brick-and-mortar outlets, among other location based services. While traditionally online and offline retailers were often enemies, in China the rapid growth of ecommerce and mobile shopping had encouraged tie-ups. Alibaba invested 4.3 billion USD in Suning, a household electrical appliances vendor, and 736 million USD in Intime retail, one of the largest shopping mall operators in China.

Alibaba almost invested in every corner of the Internet field, including social networking services (SNS) Momo and Weibo (also known as the Twitter in China), location based services like GPS navigation AutoNavi (in Chinese: Gaodeditu) and Kuaidi Taxi, online traveling agency qyer.com, online sports event data provider Sportradar, Internet security service supplier LBE Security, data analysis service company umeng.com, voice advertisement service company Shengmeng, and overseas mobile application development company Quixey. Alibaba invested heavily in both domestic and overseas logistic companies, including the 360 million USD investment in Haier to smooth the large goods delivery, the 249 million USD investment in Singapore Post to establish an international ecommerce logistic platform and a 150 million USD investment in the Hong Kong based mobile logistics platform GoGoVan.

In the category of culture and entertainment in particular film production, Alibaba acquired China Vision Media Group with 802 million USD and integrated it into its own business module named Ali Picture. Alibaba also acquired Youku Tudou online video (also known as China's YouTube) with a total valuation of 5.6 billion USD, and two online music platforms TTPOD and Xiami Music, to integrate into its own music platform named Ali Music. Moreover, Alibaba established Ali Sports to explore opportunities in the sports industry in 2015. In the category of digital healthcare, Alibaba invested in CITIC 21 CN with 170 million USD in 2014, acquired 54.3% of its stock, and renamed it AliHealth, which becomes Alibaba's digital healthcare flagship. After this acquisition, Alibaba invested in several other companies and hospitals. Last but not least, in the category of online financial services, Alibaba invested in a whole range of services, such as peer-to-peer lending, consumer loans, as well as overseas payment services in India, Thailand and South Korea.

In fact, the last transformation is accompanied by a change of investment strategy in which Alibaba had started to rapidly expand with investments both domestically and internationally. Chapter 3 will specifically deal with Alibaba's growth by investment strategy and Chapter 9 will compare its strategy to Baidu, Tencent, Xiaomi and LeEco. Although investments and acquisitions dominate, alliances and partnership also play a role, such as the collaboration between Rural Taobao and AGCO, a US leader in the design, manufacture and distribution of agricultural

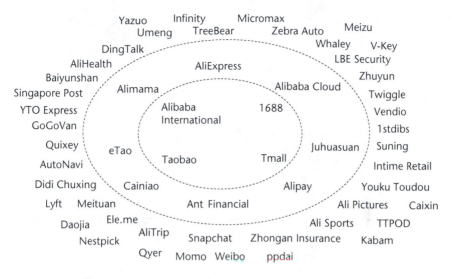

FIGURE 2.5 Alibaba ecosystem (selected examples in third layer)

Source: author's own figure.

machinery and solutions (Erickson, 2015). All in all, Alibaba developed a complex and dynamic business ecosystem, as illustrated by Figure 2.5.

2.6 Insights: Proactive transformation into a diversified business ecosystem

Alibaba attributes its success largely to the business ecosystem it is fostering. In particular, the continuous transformation of Alibaba's business ecosystem ensures an increasingly better satisfaction of customer needs and better fit into the changing business context. The transformations have included:

- B2B, C2C to B2C diversification within ecommerce business and extending SME client services, expanding consumer services, consolidating and upgrading;
- Transforming from pure ecommerce to a whole digital empire, diversification outside of ecommerce by creating new nodes in the financial sector, social networking services, digital health, and culture and entertainment;
- Transformation includes not only successes but also fraud scandals of 2011 and business failures of, for instance, Laiwang instant messaging and Yahoo! China;
- From organic growth to intensive investment based expansion. The first 12 years of Alibaba's growth are characterized as an organic growth aiming to build a strong interdependent ecosystem. It was in 2012 that Alibaba's growth approach started to shift and by 2013 the investment expansion mode was the dominant growth mechanism.

The business ecosystem of Alibaba is characterized by at least five features:

1. Digital driven: The use of advanced information and communication technology allows customers to search anything they want from a wide range of products in an electronic marketplace. The reputation and feedback mechanism in combination with live chat communication between the buyer and seller ensures reliability and trust. Due to the comprehensive ecosystem of services, clients can negotiate prices, transactions, logistics and delivery time, all at low cost. Creating mutual benefit at low cost, any new partner can join this business network;

2. Interdependence of businesses: The ecommerce businesses cross-sell and cross-market each other's services and offer packaged deals. Moreover, the core ecommerce system and the second layer of the ecosystem are mutually dependent, i.e. without the core the second layer cannot function optimally but also the other way around, without the outer layer, the core cannot provide a comprehensive offering. Lastly, even the third layer of diversified businesses are interdependent with Alibaba's other ecosystem businesses as all of the businesses in the third layer are partly owned or invested by an Alibaba business. Moreover, since the businesses are strategically synergistic, value and business can be created for one another. Economies of scale are created by the large user base of shoppers at the core of the ecosystem and the shared services such as online payment (Alipay), data services (Alibaba Cloud), smart logistics (Cainiao) and communication (Aliwangwang);

3. A focal player: How well the platform attracts participants, both producers and consumers, and supply and demand is largely dependent on Alibaba's core platforms. Enlarged by the importance of Alipay's, Alibaba Cloud's shared services and increasingly Cainiao's logistics network, the business ecosystem is to some extent orchestrated by the focal platforms, while allowing a wide variety of experiments and dynamics;

4. Co-evolution of the ecosystem with the business context: While business transformation is often forced by internal financial difficulties or external forces such as regulation, technology and markets, the case of Alibaba shows that the transformation of its business ecosystem is not just a response to internal or external forces but rather an ongoing and proactive transformation. The business ecosystem is first organically fitting itself into the business context and building up a functioning business ecosystem that meets the demands of the market and, then, at a later stage orchestrating the transformation of the business context, opening up new markets, exploring technologies and niches, such as in Internet finance and digital healthcare. The strategic change is not forced by the business context, rather, the business ecosystem is co-evolving with its context;

5. Cross industry diversification: The scope of the business activities within Alibaba's business ecosystem is wide. The business ecosystem has not only diversified its core business in ecommerce, such as moving from B2B to C2C

markets or internationalizing with cross border ecommerce, it has also diversified beyond the ecommerce industry. In particular, Alibaba has surprised many incumbent MNCs in traditional industries such as finance, healthcare, logistics, moviemaking, travel, by entering these industries with new and often disruptive service offerings. Cross industry diversification appears to be a key feature and the source of a competitive advantage of Alibaba's business ecosystem.

The strategic change of Alibaba's business ecosystem begs the question of how such transformation and growth was facilitated. Clearly, the transformation has been proactive rather than reactive, which is unusual in the business world (Johnson et al., 2012). In other words, how did Alibaba succeed in this wholesale transformation? The answer lies in Alibaba's adoption of four growth models: 1) investment, 2) incubation, 3) innovation and 4) internationalization. The next four chapters will discuss each of these growth strategies.

References

Alibaba Group, 2016 *Alibaba Group Financial Reports 2016*, Hong Kong, Alibaba Group. Available at: http://www.alibabagroup.com/en/ir/secfilings. Accessed 22/02/2017.

Clark, D., 2016 *Alibaba: The house that Jack Ma built*, New York, Ecco.

Erisman, P., 2015 *Alibaba's world: How a remarkable Chinese company is changing the face of global business*, New York, St. Martin's Press.

Erickson, J.,2015. AGCO, *Alibaba Help Advance China Farming*. Alizila.com. Available at: http://www.alizila.com/agco-alibaba-help-advance-china-farming/, Accessed 22/12/2016.

Greeven, M.J., 2014. 'Alibaba group and Jack Ma', In Yu, F.L. Yan, H.D. Yan, ed. *Handbook in East Asia Entrepreneurship*, Chap. 33. London, Routledge.

Greeven, M.J., Yang, S., Heck, E. and Krug, B., 2010., 'The ecosystem of the Alibaba Group: How is Alibaba Group's strategy and implementation in China creating sustainable value for suppliers, partners and customers?', *The Case Centre*, Reference no. 310-125-1-2.

Greeven, M.J., Yang, S.Y., Yue, T., Van Heck, E. and Krug, B., 2012., 'How Taobao bested eBay in China', *Financial Times*, 12 March.

Johnson, G., Yip, G.S. and Hensmans, M., 2012.. Achieving successful strategic transformation. *MIT Sloan Management Review*, [online] Available at: http://sloanreview.mit.edu/article/achieving-successful-strategic-transformation/. Accessed 12/02/2017.

3

EXPANDING BY INVESTING

Speeding up the growth of Alibaba's business ecosystem

3.1 Introduction

Alibaba's taste for growth is relentless. Since 2013 Alibaba moved from organic growth to high speed growth by investing in and acquiring companies in sectors such as ecommerce, logistics, location based services, finance, healthcare, travel and entertainment. What drove this transformation in Alibaba's growth strategy? How did Alibaba's investments and acquisitions lead to value creation? How are the diversified investments connected to Alibaba's core business? In this chapter, we will draw on our BATXL database to discuss Alibaba's investments and provide a comprehensive overview of the investment sectors, location and target companies growth phase. Moreover, we will highlight several investments that represent investments in different phases of the target companies' growth and in different sectors. Specifically, we discuss the effects of this growth strategy for Alibaba's ecosystem. In the last section we conclude with a discussion on the regulatory context for investment in China as a key factor influencing this growth approach.

3.2 From organic growth to high speed growth by investment

The first decade of Alibaba's growth has been organic, aiming to build an ecosystem of ecommerce companies. Meanwhile, Alibaba also broadly collaborated with various external partners to seek further growth. For instance, Alibaba partnered with CITIC Bank to offer a quick payment function for Alipay and collaborated with the Bank of Communications to offer lending products to SMEs. Moreover, Alibaba also already invested in other companies, particularly in complementary ecommerce services. For instance, Alibaba invested in Baozun, an integrated ecommerce solution provider for online retailers, OneTouch (in Chinese: Yidatong), a one stop import and export SME services provider; Taotaosou, an online products search and price comparison tool; and Vendio, Alibaba's first overseas acquisition, a company that offers retailers software services to smooth their online operations. Moreover, Alibaba acquired ecommerce competitors such as Yipai. Then, in 2012 Alibaba's growth approach started to shift and by 2013 growth by investment was without doubt the dominant growth mechanism.

Since 2013, both the number of investments and the amount per investment showed an unprecedented increase (see Figure 3.1). Most of the investments were highly diversified in terms of investment round (see Figure 3.2), target countries (see Figure 3.4) and in diverse sectors (see Section 3.3 and Figure 3.5). In what follows we will discuss what fuels these investments, the increase of investment deals, investment rounds, target countries and investment sectors.

3.2.1 What fuels Alibaba's investments?

The change in growth strategy from organic growth to growth by investment is fuelled by Alibaba's strong financial position and financing capability. By 2013, Alibaba had reached a capacity of financial capital available that allowed them to significantly grow by investment. In particular, Alibaba's financial strength comes from several sources: 1) a strong business cash flow securing 5.6 billion USD in profits in 2015 alone; 2) outstanding financing capability, including its historic IPO in September 2014 (25 billion USD), large corporate bond issued in November 2014 (8 billion USD) as well as other forms of financial leverage such as bank loans (in March 2016, 8 billion USD short term debt); 3) considering the cash flow position of Alibaba's profitable businesses in combination with its financing capability, Alibaba has also become an attractive co-investor for many funds and companies. Therefore, many of the investments are not exclusively done by Alibaba but in collaboration with other investors.

3.2.2 Boom of investment deals

The number of Alibaba's investments has increased significantly in the last years and at least three features stand out (see Figure 3.1):

1. Exponential growth until 2015, a total growth of about 16 times from 2012 to 2015; however, the growth is similar to Alibaba's peer companies (see Chapter 8);
2. It's not only the growth but also the absolute number of deals that is striking: compared to companies from the US or Europe, the average number of investment deals per company is high;
3. Slowdown in 2016, but of course the absolute number of 39 deals is still remarkable.

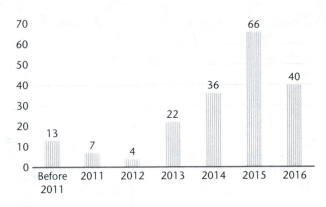

FIGURE 3.1 Alibaba's investments by year (# of deals)

Source: authors' own BATXL database.

The investment in such a significant number of companies suggests an overall boost of the growth of the business ecosystem, where about 150 new participants entered in just four years' time. Moreover, it clearly shows the ambition of Alibaba to be more than an ecommerce ecosystem. While the growth is fuelled by a strategic ambition not unknown in China's Internet sector, it also raises questions of how the invested companies and their products, technologies and brands can be usefully integrated into Alibaba's ecosystem. In fact, traditional research on a company's investment and acquisition activity would suggest that there are limitations to a company's absorptive capacity, i.e. to what extent the company can not only acquire but also put to good use the newly acquired resources such as brand, people and knowledge. However, a business ecosystem is different from a company as it does not just represent one company but a whole group of interdependent companies. Moreover, as our research suggests, most of the companies invested or acquired are not merged or integrated but will stay independently run businesses. Usually, the product or service offerings are bundled, and operations are shared via services such as payment, cloud services and logistics, in addition to access to the user base.

3.2.3 From early phase investments to full acquisitions

The types of Alibaba's investments are highly diverse and at least five features stand out (see Figure 3.2):

1. Diversity of investments and no particular dominant type of investment. This is a rather different approach from both corporate VC and professional funds since they tend to have a more narrow focus. Normally speaking, corporate VC tend to look for investment targets that can eventually be merged into the company, while professional funds tend to have a specific focus in terms of both industries and phases. Nevertheless, Alibaba is not that different from its peers Tencent and Baidu; we do see clear differences with Xiaomi and LeEco. Chapter 9 will compare them in more detail;

2. 22% of the total investments was in early phase (pre A and A round); suggesting Alibaba is looking for pioneering technologies and business models;
3. The range of early phase domestic investment is from one million RMB to 70 million RMB. It is quite diverse and some of the larger A round investments could easily considered to be private equity deals;
4. Acquisitions have played a significant role, reaching about 18% of the total investment deals;
5. The range of domestic acquisition is diverse, from 10 million RMB to 40 billion RMB. See Figure 3.3 for illustrative acquisitions since 2005.

The wide variety of phases of investments from pioneering start-ups to mature and even public companies suggests a strategy of diversification and risk spreading. Moreover, this suggests that Alibaba's business ecosystem does not have the specific focus regarding the growth phase of the company that a professional fund would have in most cases. At the same time it also does not resemble the approach of a corporate venture fund which oftentimes is focused on earlier phase ventures that have the potential to be integrated into the existing business units and/or technology road map of the company. The findings suggest a rather unique investment approach for business ecosystems.

3.2.4 A Quarter of investments overseas

Alibaba's investments have not only been in China, in fact, it has been expanding its investment activity abroad; see Figure 3.4. The overseas investment started mostly in 2013, suggesting a recent trend in line with Alibaba's global ambition. By now, 23% of Alibaba's investments have been overseas, although predominantly in the

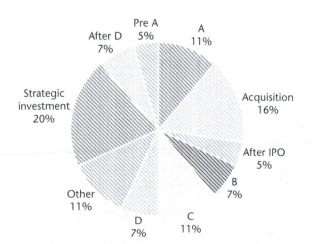

FIGURE 3.2 Alibaba's investments: round distribution (end 2016; # of deals)

Source: authors' own BATXL database.

Yahoo!	**Vendio**	**AutoNavi**	**Youku Tudou**
2005 Acquired Yahoo! China	2010 Acquired Vendio in the US (the first overseas acquisition)	2014 Acquired AutoNavi with over 1 billion USD billion USD	2015 Acquired Youku Tudou with 5.6

Wanwang	**Xiami**	**UC Web**	**Wandoujia**
2009 Acquired Zhongguowanwang with 83 million USD	2013 Acquired Xiami Music	2014 Acquired UCWeb with over 4 billion USD	2016 Acquired Wandoujia with 200 million USD

FIGURE 3.3 Illustrative acquisitions of Alibaba

Source: authors' own figure.

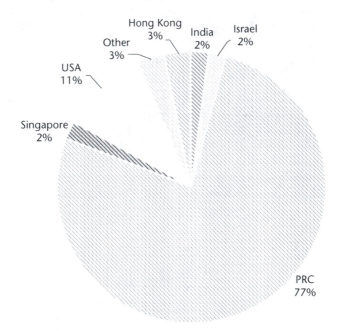

FIGURE 3.4 Alibaba's investments: geographic distribution (end 2016; # of deals)

Source: authors' own BATXL database.

USA. In this chapter, we will focus on the domestic investments. Later in Chapter 6, we will discuss Alibaba's overseas investments as part of Alibaba going global.

3.3 Investments in emerging high growth sectors

In our research we identify at least 23 distinct sectors of investment; see Figure 3.5. It appears that Alibaba invested in every aspect of the Internet field and there is no specific dominant sector. Nevertheless, we can identify several sectors of particular interest, such as culture and entertainment, ecommerce, location based services

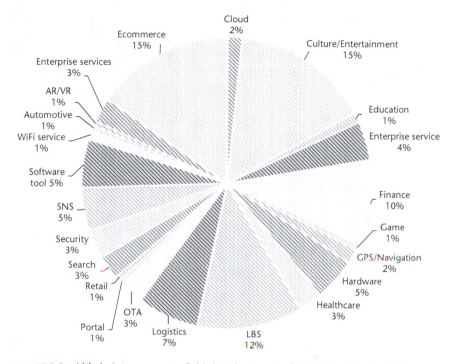

FIGURE 3.5 Alibaba's investments: field distribution (end 2016; # of deals). LBS: Location Based Services; OTA: Online Travel Agent; AR/VR: Augmented Reality or Virtual Reality; SNS: Social Network Service

Source: authors' own BATXL database.

(LBS), finance and enterprise services. Moreover, recent investments include new important strategic areas such as digital healthcare and logistics. As we will show, these sectors are all high growth sectors in China.

Culture and entertainment: In film production, Alibaba acquired China Vision Media Group for 800 million USD and integrated it into its own business to establish Ali Pictures. Furthermore, Alibaba made a significant strategic investment in Huayi Bros. Media Group. Actually, both Alibaba and Tencent are investors in Huayi which is one of the largest media groups in China. In term of news media, Alibaba acquired *Hong Kong South China Morning Post* for 266 million USD, and made strategic investments in the financial news media Yicai. Another large acquisition in culture and entertainment is the acquisition of Youku Tudou, known as China's YouTube, with a total valuation of 5.6 billion USD, which at that time broke the record of acquisition amount in the Internet industry. Alibaba also acquired two online music platforms TTPOD (in Chinese: Tiantiandongting) and Xiami Music to integrate into its own music platform named Ali Music. The culture and entertainment targets of Alibaba's investments have seen significant and large scale acquisitions and by now Alibaba's ecosystem has a stronghold on the booming entertainment industry in China. The prospects for the entertainment industry in China are great (see Table 3.1) and China has already a dozen or so billionaires,

TABLE 3.1 Key investments and booming Chinese sectors

Sector	Alibaba's investments	Sector growth indicators
Culture and entertainment	15% of total; 29 deals	70% average annual growth of movie tickets sales from 2010–2015
Ecommerce	15% of total; 29 deals	60% average annual growth of online sales volume from 2011–2015
LBS	12% of total; 22 deals	200% average annual growth of market size from 2011–2015
Financial services	10% of total; 18 deals	154% average annual growth of online financial product market size
Enterprise services	4% of total; 8 deals	85% average annual growth of enterprise services market size from 2014–2016
Digital healthcare	3% of total; 5 deals	50% average annual growth of digital healthcare market size from 2012–2016 and predicted to increase
Logistics	7% of total; 13 deals	Over 50% average annual growth of express delivery of packages from 2011–2016

Sources: Data compiled from Chinese data providers China Industry Information (2016a, 2016b); CECRC (2016); China Business Intelligence Net (2015); EC (2016); iHeima (2015); Analysys (2016).

including Tencent's Ma Huateng and LeEco's Jia Yueting, who made their fortunes in entertainment industries like film, TV, online media and games (Forbes, 2015).

Ecommerce: ecommerce has been and is still the core of Alibaba. The rise of Alibaba is basically in parallel with the boom of China's ecommerce. Together with the organic growth of its ecommerce business, from Alibaba.com and 1688.com to Taobao, Tmall and AliExpress, it also never stopped investing. The earliest acquisition was in 2005 when Alibaba bought Yahoo! China. Later its investment targets also included companies like net.cn (in Chinese: Zhongguowanwang) and Taoqiao which offer one stop solution for ecommerce of SMEs, or Yinman and Artka, which are pure ecommerce apparel brands. Moreover, Alibaba's investments in ecommerce also extended to the USA, India, Hong Kong and Singapore. In particular, the US appears to be a key market for Alibaba. American ecommerce platforms like 1stdibs, Zulily, Jet.com and ecommerce service providers like Vendio and Shopex were all invested by Alibaba. In total, there are 29 deals in ecommerce, occupying about 15% of its whole investments portfolio. The prospects for global ecommerce are good and with Alibaba, larger than Amazon and eBay combined, China is a frontrunner (Forbes, 2014); see Table 3.1.

Location based services: LBS is a strategic priority for the Alibaba. On one hand, the on-demand economy is geared to deliver greater convenience to consumers and more sales opportunities for retailers and service providers by combining mobile Internet technology with traditional stores. On the other hand, not satisfied with just running online shopping marketplaces, Alibaba aims to enable and support an expanding range of commercial activities, such as paying electronically in offline shops, ordering movie tickets and take-out noodles, booking transportation, and buying merchandise online but picking their orders up at brick-and-mortar outlets. For instance, Alibaba invested 4.3 billion USD in Suning, a household electrical appliances vendor, and 736 million USD in Intime retail, one of the largest shopping mall operators in China. Alibaba teams up with old-school retailers and tried to leverage each other's strengths to introduce new, mobile technology enabled products and services. By now Alibaba's ecommerce ecosystem is dominating Chinese online market places; the end of LBS sector is not yet in sight, as it is still expanding in China (see Table 3.1).

Finance: Alibaba started its investment in the financial sector in 2013 with lots of media attention and promotion. Alibaba co-founded Zhongan Insurance with Tencent and Pingan Insurance, while in order to release the monetary market fund product served with Alipay, i.e. Yu'ebao, Alibaba also invested 180 million USD in Tianhong Fund Management and co-developed Yu'ebao later. Then, Alibaba invested in peer to peer lending (P2P) company ppdai.com, which was one of the most popular business trends in the Internet finance sector in China. After Alibaba established its finance arm, Ant Financial Group, Ant Financial invested in qufenqi. com (Internet consumer lending and installment), Tianjin Financial Asset Exchange and Postal Saving Bank of China domestically, as well as Paytm in India, K Bank in South Korea, Ascend Money in Thailand and, in February 2017, in Mynt in the Philippines. Moreover, Ant Financial has acquired the US listed money transfer network MoneyGram. Since Alibaba's online financial services have become a large part of the ecosystem, and to some extent, started a new sub-ecosystem, we discuss Alibaba's investments in finance ventures in more detail and in context of their own developments and partnerships in Chapter 5. The sector is booming in China and Alibaba has been competing extensively with other Internet companies for the market, such as Tencent, Baidu, Xiaomi, LeEco and JD. According to the World Economic Forum 2017, half of all investments in financial technology is happening in Asia, especially China.

Enterprise services: Alibaba not only serves millions of online shoppers (both individuals and businesses) but also serves millions of SMEs which open their shops on the platforms of Alibaba. By developing SME client services such as Alimama and Alibaba Cloud, Alibaba helps SMEs to develop their online business, while at the same time increasing its own profitability. The deep understanding of SMEs' demands later also facilitated Alibaba in its investment in enterprise services. By investing in the marketing service providers like Ad China, ShengMeng and CRM providers like YaZuo, Alibaba is also proactively building a better ecosystem for their SME clients.

Besides the current significant position in various sectors, Alibaba has laid out a clear strategy to be part of the digital healthcare disruption and committed to co-develop a smart logistics system. In the digital healthcare sector, Alibaba invested in CITIC 21 CN with 170 million USD in 2014, acquired 54.3% of its stock, and renamed it AliHealth, which became Alibaba's digital healthcare flagship. The acquisition of CITIC 21 CN allowed Alibaba to obtain a pilot license to sell medicine on Tmall and moreover, set foot in China's drug data analytics sector. In 2008, China Food and Drug Administration established a supervision code for every box of drug on sale, to supervise the whole process of the drug from production to retail. This supervision system was developed and run exclusively by CITIC 21 CN, and the data has been stored in Alibaba Cloud after the acquisition. Later on, Alibaba invested in Baiyunshan, a pharmaceutical company; Huakang Mobile Healthcare, an online hospital appointment reservation platform; and Wanli Cloud, a medical image big data and cloud company to broaden its business into the digital health sector. Again, this is a booming industry, not only in China but worldwide, and Alibaba is aiming to be part of it, as evidenced in Table 3.1.

In the smart logistics sector, Alibaba invested heavily in both domestic and overseas logistic companies. In close connection to the ecommerce boom in China, the express delivery industry is on a gold rush (*Financial Times*, 2017). Alibaba is trying to be part of the logistics boom and drive new smart logistics, i.e. big data driven logistics, initiatives. Their investments include a 360 million USD investment in Haier to smooth large goods delivery and the 249 million USD investment in Singapore Post to establish an international ecommerce logistic platform and a 150 million USD investment in the Hong Kong based mobile logistics platform GoGoVan. Alibaba also invested several express delivery providers, such as Best Logistics (in Chinese: Baishiwuliu), Star Express (in Chinese: Xingchenjibian) and YTO Express (in Chinese: Yuantongkuaidi). In a broader strategy to develop a smart logistics network (Cainiao), these investments are facilitating Alibaba's hold on logistics (see Section 4.3). In general, the logistics sector in China is developing rapidly and with increased automation and upgrading of the industry, the market prospects seem to be good, as evidenced in Table 3.1.

All in all, with this more detailed look at the specific sectors Alibaba invested in, we can conclude that the investments have led into significant diversification. From the above investment analysis it also becomes clear that the third layer of Alibaba's ecosystem (see Section 2.5) is most of all the result of extensive investments. The investment logic is to some extent mirroring that of a professional investment fund, i.e. focusing on high growth sectors. However, unlike professional investment funds, Alibaba has a wide scope of sectors and no particular preference for investing in specific growth phases of ventures. Moreover, Alibaba's approach is not following a corporate venturing approach which is characterized by, generally, a technology and market road map and clear strategic specifications. So, here it appears that the investment logic of a business ecosystem is quite unique. In the following section, we will discuss several spotlight cases from different sectors and stages of investment and assess the financial and strategic impact on the business ecosystem of Alibaba.

3.4 Spotlight cases: Successful investments

The following spotlight cases highlight six investments from Alibaba in a variety of sectors and in different rounds of investment. For each case we discuss how the investment has affected Alibaba's business ecosystem and how successful the investment was from both a professional investor perspective and from a business ecosystem perspective. Table 3.2 provides a comparison of the spotlight cases in terms of Alibaba's investment, financial results and impact on the business ecosystem.

3.4.1 Momo: Social network services

Momo is one of the most popular mobile social tools in China. It was founded by Tang Yan in March 2011 and launched the first product five months later. It is a location based mobile app which can facilitate users to know who are in the vicinity and also using Momo at the same time. Within one year, it attracted over 10 million users with over 40 million messages delivered in the network.

TABLE 3.2 Spotlight cases: impact on Alibaba's business ecosystem

Company	Sector	Commitment	Results	Business ecosystem	Time frame
Momo	Social network services	B and C round	IPO	Re-enter mobile social space	2012–2015
YTO Express	Logistics	Pre IPO	IPO	Reduce dependence and enter smart logistics	2015–2016
Intime	Offline retail	Strategic investment	Privatization	Diversify into offline business segment	2014–2017
Meizu	Hardware electronics	Strategic investment	Fivefold growth	Entry smartphone hardware	2015–2016
Youku Tudou	Culture and entertainment	Strategic investment	Privatization	Absorption into the business ecosystem	2014–2016
Yazuo	Enterprise services	C round	N/A	Extension of existing services	2015–now

Alibaba always has had the ambition to expand its influence in the digital social field. While its own mobile social product Laiwang failed, the total 25 million USD investment in Momo in 2012 (B round) and 2013 (C round) seems successful. The registered users reached 150 million by 2014 and Momo was listed in NASDAQ in the same year. The company achieved 130 million USD revenue and over 30 million USD net profit in 2015. Here we can see a case in which Alibaba's business ecosystem has successfully entered the mobile social space and the investment, which was in the relatively mature phase, paid off with a successful IPO.

3.4.2 YTO express: Logistics

China's express delivery industry grew up together with the rapid development of the ecommerce industry. China had already become the largest express delivery country with over 20 billion packages delivered in 2015. After ten years of development and consolidation, China's top five private express delivery companies clearly stand out: SF Express, YTO Express, ZTO Express, STO Express and Yunda Express. As the dominant player in China's ecommerce industry, Alibaba's relationship with the express delivery companies has always been complicated: on one hand, the express delivery companies rely on deals brought by Alibaba's ecommerce; on the other hand, Alibaba's profitable business also relies on express delivery companies. Alibaba understands the importance of its logistics suppliers. Its Ciaoniao project is one way to build up logistics capabilities like data, infrastructure and warehouses. The strategic investment to YTO Express in 2015, is another way to involve directly in logistics. YTO Express successfully went public by listing on the domestic stock exchange in 2016, which also made Alibaba's investment a typical pre-IPO case. Observers see the YTO deal not only as a successful investment, but also as a way for Alibaba to slightly reduce their dependence on external express delivery companies.

3.4.3 Intime: Offline retail

As the largest player in China's ecommerce industry, disrupting offline retail was once the mission of Alibaba. However, after over a decade of high speed growth of online retail in China, saturation is in sight; especially with transformations from C2C to B2C, from domestic to cross border ecommerce, from urban to rural areas. In the Ali Yunqi Conference in October 2016, Ma Yun indicated the end of China's 'pure ecommerce time'. Alibaba's Yunqi Conference is one of the largest cloud computing summits in the world. According to Ma Yun, there will not be ecommerce, there will only be new retail, which means retail must combine online, offline and logistics. In fact, in March 2014, Alibaba already strategically invested 5.7 billion HKD to Intime, one of the most well known department stores and shopping mall chains in Zhejiang Province (listed on the Hong Kong Stock Exchange since 2007). Since then, Alibaba and Intime started several collaborations in retail.

In January 2017, Alibaba and the founder of Intime, Shen Guojun, announced that they plan to privatize Intime, which means Alibaba will hold over 70% of Intime's shares after the privatization. At the same time, Alibaba also invested in Suning (one of China's largest electric appliance stores) and Sanjiang (a supermarket chain in Zhejiang Province) to further explore a more optimized retail experience, better integrating online and offline retail resources for consumers. With the investment and subsequent privatization of Intime, Alibaba's business ecosystem has taken the next step to diversify into offline retail and increase impact on offline business.

3.4.4 Meizu: Hardware electronics

Alibaba is a digital giant: it was born in the Internet wave at the beginning of twenty-first century and rose with the digitalizing trend of the whole country. In general, most of the companies Alibaba invested in are digital or software companies. However, there are also exceptions and 2014–2015 was a period were many Internet giants turned their attention to hardware ventures. In February 2015, Alibaba invested in Meizu, one of the top ten Chinese smartphone providers, with about 600 million USD. With this, Alibaba has made its first significant domestic entry into the hardware consumer electronics industry; in addition to their overseas hardware investments and domestic investments in Internet TV, pads and smart robots companies. Meizu was established in 2003 by Huang Zhang. This company achieved a big success as a domestic market leader for MP3 players and transformed to a mobile phone company afterwards. Its first phone product was launched in 2009 and Meizu became top ten domestic smartphone brands within two years. Considering the connectivity and complementarity of two companies' fields, the strategic collaboration is not strange. In particular, since Alibaba launched its own operation system YunOS in 2011 to enter the deeper infrastructure of mobile technology which is increasingly important considering connectivity between online and offline. In the past years it keeps upgrading and promoting it. However, according to observers, without understanding hardware technology, it is not easy for an OS to achieve real success. The investment of Meizu will certainly allow a deeper collaboration between YunOS and Meizu phone. While we do not know yet how successful the investment is from a financial perspective, Meizu's phone shipment has increased from 4 to 22 million by the end of 2016, indicating a significant growth of business.

3.4.5 Youku Tudou: Online entertainment

Together with the economic development and boom of the middle class, the entertainment industry is growing at an unprecedented pace. At the same time, all kinds of entertainment such as TV, movies, games and music are being digitalized. Considering the huge market potential as well as the direct connection with the digital world, it is not strange that Alibaba is eager to step into it. Youku was established in 2006 and listed on New York Stock Exchange in 2010 while Tudou was founded in 2005 and listed on NASDAQ in 2011. At that time, Youku and Tudou were the two largest video platforms in China. They merged and reached a combined 400 million monthly active users in 2012 and have been known as China's Youtube ever since. In May 2014, Alibaba invested 1.2 billion USD into Youku Tudou and one year later privatized the whole company. Currently, Youku Tudou has all kinds of collaborations within Alibaba's business ecosystem, such as content delivery network development together with Alibaba Cloud, and 'video shopping' (shopping while watching video) project together with Alimama, among others. With this large scale acquisition, Alibaba's business ecosystem has solidified a position in online entertainment by merging an established player into its ecosystem.

3.4.6 Yazuo: Enterprise services

Established in 2006, Yazuo currently is one of the largest SaaS CRM providers for the catering industry in China with about 50 IT engineers. It is now serving about 200,000 catering brands such as Quanjude, Zhouheiya and Zoo Coffee in over 200 Chinese cities, aiming to help the catering operators to know their consumers better and manage their relationship better. After analyzing both online and offline data collected from the client, precision marketing will be offered by the company to help stores improve their performance, and what is more important is that it can offer a direct interface to Alibaba's LBS network. In June 2015, Ant Financial, the financial services arm of Alibaba's business ecosystem, did a C round investment in Yazuo, in order to expand its LBS ecosystem. The investment in Yazuo is a strategic move for Alibaba to expand the new Koubei, i.e. location based services platform, and it also follows a trend of expanding SME client services that started with Alibaba's development of Alisoft in 2007 and many other developments (see Section 2.4).

3.5 China's regulatory context and the equity investment boom

In order to understand and assess the investment boom of Alibaba, it is important to consider the broader regulatory context for private investments in China. As mentioned in Chapter 1, regulation is both a source of concern and a source of opportunity. Therefore, we need to understand the above developments in China's regulatory context and to what extent the current growth strategy by investment is sustainable in the long term from a regulatory point of view.

   China's first law related to investment funds was issued in 1998. Before that, there was no formal private investment industry whatsoever in the country. However, the investment industry was relatively passive from 1999 to 2010, despite the ongoing developments in the capital market and maturity of the regulatory environment. Until 2005 there are only about 500 VC/PE investment institutions active, in comparison to over 10,000 in 2015. Several important developments in the regulatory environment to promote private investment include: the first foreign VC provision (2001), the launch of Shenzhen SME capital market (2004), the measures for the administration of VC investment enterprises (2005), the relaunch of China's IPO application (2006), and the launch of ChiNext, i.e. China's NASDAQ (2009).

It was not until 2010 that China's investment industry took off. In concordance with the twelfth Five-year Plan, the government issued opinions on encouraging and guiding the development of private investment and policy on the taxation of equity investment funds. Meanwhile, the State Council issued the decision on accelerating the development of strategic emerging industries, i.e. new generation information technology, biotechnology, new material, high end equipment manufacturing, and new energy. The explicitly positive signal from the government gave the equity investment industry a push besides the prosperity of the domestic capital market. According to Zero2IPO China's VC/PE 2015 Market Review, since 2011, the funds raised and invested (in particular RMB funds), the number of deals as well as VC/PE firms all indicated the vitality boom of China's investment industry. The overall number of deals and investment amount in 2015 is the highest since the previous high of 2011; right before, potential overheating led to a closing of the domestic IPO market. By 2015 there were about 8,500 VE/PE investment deals, up from 450 in 2006 representing a value of 500 billion RMB. Along came a series of relevant regulations and policies on the investment industry and capital markets, but there was a drawback in 2012–2013 when new IPOs were prohibited for over a year, thereby limiting exit options for especially private equity investors.

Then, according to observers, 2015 was another crucial year for equity investment: the Chinese government declared several significant decisions and policies to promote entrepreneurship and innovation. The government announced a 40 billion RMB VC guidance fund for emerging industries and reform of systems and mechanisms to accelerate implementation of innovation driven development strategies; the development of incubators is strongly supported to promote mass innovation and business start-ups. In particular, 'Internet plus' as a key driver of economy, has been mentioned and promoted in the government work report. Not surprisingly, the VC investment in Internet related industries again dominated the market. In particular, we see several key target industries for investors, both in terms of number of deals and investment amount, including Internet, telecom, IT, bio-healthcare and finance. Those top target industries are not only quite in line with the promotional policies and regulations of the Chinese government but also, according to observers, with the specific market needs, driven mostly by digital technologies.

The merger and acquisition (M&A) market is also growing along with the investment industry in China. Especially in 2015, a total of 2,692 acquisitions, with a trading volume of 1 trillion RMB were completed, an increase of about 40% compared with 2014, according to Zero2IPO. In August 2015, the Chinese government issued a notice on encouraging mergers, acquisitions and restructuring to further streamline administration and delegate powers to lower levels.

This also greatly improved the M&A market. If we look at the industry breakdown of M&A in 2015, over 40% of M&As were in just four sectors: Internet, telecom, bio-health tech and IT. Internet is again eye-catching, which was mostly invested by digital incumbents like BAT. Moreover, it is interesting to note that while the number of cross border M&A deals by Chinese companies are rising only slowly, the amount of overseas investment deals is significant and on average larger than domestic M&A deals.

Summarizing, the regulatory conditions for investments, VC/PE but also merger and acquisitions have significantly improved and the regulatory guidelines have in particular stimulated investment activities in Internet related industries. Moreover, the 2015 government VC support fund and associated policies to promote entrepreneurship and new venturing are supportive and in line with Alibaba's growth by investment strategy.

3.6 Insights: Emergent investment approach

Alibaba has grown from an apartment start-up to one of the world's largest Internet companies within less than two decades. Alibaba grew quickly in a fast growing market and driven by the Internet boom, upgrading of the middle class and an increasingly supportive regulatory environment, especially for equity investments. However, organic growth was not enough to keep up with the market and ambition of the company. Alibaba expanded quickly through investment and acquisition in particular since 2013. During this period, Alibaba's competitors in China began to follow a similar growth strategy, which further intensified the competition and sped up the expansion. The features of Alibaba's investments and acquisitions can be summarized as follows:

- Strong financing capability. Note that Alibaba's investments often leverage bank loans (8 billion USD short term debt in March 2016), co-investors, and connected to its historic IPO in 2014 (25 billion USD) and large company bond issue (8 billion USD) in the same year. Moreover, the highly profitable business also brings in a lot of cash every year (5.6 billion USD in 2015);
- Exponential growth until 2015, a total growth of about 16 times from 2012 to 2015, reaching 188 deals by 2016;
- Most of the investment targets were domestic entrepreneurial Internet related enterprises and most of the investments were either early stage pre A and A investments or later stage acquisitions and after IPO investments;
- Most of the investments were made in mainland China. Among Alibaba's overseas investments, about 45% are in the US;
- In terms of sectors, before 2013, Alibaba's investments concentrated on ecommerce, including ecommerce support, logistics and ecommerce related enterprise services. Since 2013, Alibaba shifted its focus and diversified into a variety of businesses, such as financial services, social networking services, digital healthcare, culture and entertainment;

- In contrast to a corporate investment fund, Alibaba's business ecosystem has a variety of investment entities, both Alibaba businesses like AliHealth, Ant Financial, Cainiao and its corporate venture funds.

Generally speaking investment and acquisition is a common approach for companies to grow and diversify. Classic strategic management focuses on motives, investment logic and outcomes. Taking a business ecosystem as a unit of analysis, instead of a company, how does this growth by investment strategy work out?

The change to grow by investment was driven by the need for increasing over-all market power in a highly competitive environment and following a strategy of pre-emptive attack. The ecosystem prioritizes speed and occupying significant positions and influence in emerging sectors, rather than focusing on direct profit-ability or absorbing the newly acquiring competences, knowledge and brands into the organization. Moreover, increased diversification is reducing the dependence on the ecommerce core business and allows exploring new sources of growth and revenue such as in financial services, digital healthcare, smart logistics, LBS and culture and entertainment industries, as Table 3.3 summarizes. Our six spotlight cases (Table 3.2) illustrate that the investments were not only financial successes but also affected the business ecosystem either by entry in newly emerging sectors or by reducing dependencies.

What is the logic of this investment approach? In order to understand the logic of Alibaba's business ecosystem investment, in contrast to a company or investment fund, we first need to distinguish two phases. In the first phase, until roughly 2012, Alibaba has had a clear and planned investment approach which focused on building and upgrading the ecommerce ecosystem, as discussed in Chapter 2. In the second phase, Alibaba is no longer following a specific plan but is almost exclusively driven by (digital) opportunities in the market. In particular, Alibaba successfully entered several emerging, high growth sectors (see Section 3.3). Our spotlight cases also show why the investments by Alibaba in those highly diverse industries actually follow a logic and how synergies are created. Moreover, as in the case of, for instance, Internet finance, movie business and digital health-care, it is a story of first following a market opportunity and once proven, each newly created node in the ecosystem will have its own investment plan within specific sectoral boundaries; see Table 3.4 for a summary of Alibaba's investment approach.

TABLE 3.3 Alibaba's motives for growth by investment strategy

• Need for speed: market growth and competition	• Increase market power
• Pre-emptive attack: fight off competition	• Reduce dependencies: diversify risks
• Explore new markets	• Ambition

TABLE 3.4 Alibaba's emergent investment approach in two phases

Phase 1 (1999–2013)	Phase 2 (2013–2017)
• **Planned investment**	• **Emergent investment**
ecommerce focus	1. Opportunity driven sectors
	2. New strategic nodes
	3. Planned approach per node

Therefore, the investment logic mirrors that of a professional investment fund, i.e. focusing on growth opportunities and emerging sectors, rather than those that are directly within the current scope of the company's capability. However, unlike professional investment funds, Alibaba has a wide scope of sectors and invests in ventures in different growth phases. Moreover, Alibaba's approach is not following a corporate venturing approach which is characterized by, generally, a technology and market road map and clear strategic specifications. Rather, the analysis suggests that growth by investment of a business ecosystem currently follows a rather unique approach that is an emergent investment rather than a planned approach such as of professional funds and corporate venturing. It must be noted that Alibaba's international investments have different features and appear to be similar to a more planned approach, as we will explore in detail in Chapter 6.

References

Analysys, 2016. 2016 nian zhong guo yi dong yi liao shi chang qu shi yu ce [2016 China mobile healthcare market trend prediction]. Available at: http://www.askci.com/news/chanye/2016/01/27/152547zn4h.shtml. Accessed 30/03/2016 [in Chinese].

CECRC, 2016. 2015 nian du zhong guo dian zi shang wu shi chang shu ju [2015 China ecommerce market data]. *China Electronic Commerce Research Center.* Available at: http://b2b.toocle.com/zt/2015ndbg/. Accessed 30/03/2016 [in Chinese].

China Business Intelligence Net, 2015. 2015 shang ban nian O2O shi chang gui mo chao 3000 yi tong bu zeng 8 cheng [First half of 2015 O2O market size over 300 billion RMB, year on year increase of eight times]. Available at: http://www.askci.com/news/2015/09/30/93430yla2.shtml. Accessed 30/03/2016 [in Chinese].

China Industry Information, 2016a. 2015 nian wo guo dian ying piao fang xin yi lun zeng zhang fen xi [2015 China movie ticket increase analysis]. Available at: http://www.chyxx.com/industry/201603/390563.html. Accessed 30/06/2016 [in Chinese].

China Industry Information, 2016b. 2016 nian zhong guo kuai di hang ye fa zhan qu shi ji ji zhong du fen xi [2016 China express delivery industry development trend and summary analysis]. Available at: http://www.chyxx.com/industry/201612/473672.html. Accessed 30/12/2016 [in Chinese].

EC, 2016. 2016 nian (shang) zhong guo hu liang wang jin rong shi chang shu ju jian ce bao gao [First half 2016 China Internet finance market data report]. *China International ecommerce Net.* Available at: http://www.ec.com.cn/article/dsyj/dsbg/201609/11985_1.html. Accessed 30/03/2016 [in Chinese].

Forbes, 2015. China's Entertainment Billionaires: China's 'Disney,' Cai Dongqing. Available at: https://www.forbes.com/sites/robcain/2015/06/21/chinas-entertainment-billionaires-chinas-disney-cai-dongqing/#3fc9a87017a7. Accessed 15/12/2016.

Forbes, 2014. B2B ecommerce market worth $6.7 trillion by 2020: Alibaba and China the front-runners. Available at: https://www.forbes.com/sites/sarwantsingh/2014/11/06/b2b-ecommerce-market-worth-6-7-trillion-by-2020/#3b8327df212e. Accessed 15/12/2016.

Financial Times, 2017. Deliverymen dig in to China's ecommerce gold rush. Available at: https://www.ft.com/content/850d920a-dd65-11e6-86ac-f253db7791c6, Accessed 24/02/2017

iHeima, 2015. Qi ye ji fu wu shi chang huo le, chuang ye zhe de ji hui lai le ma? [Enterprise service market heating up, is this an opportunity for entrepreneurs?]. Available at: http://www.iheima.com/space/2015/1229/153513.shtml. Accessed 30/03/2016 [in Chinese].

World Economic Forum, 2017. *The Global fintech revolution*. Available at: http://www.weforum.org/events/world-economic-forum-annual-meeting-2017/sessions/the-global-fintech-revolution. Accessed 20/02/2017.

Zero2IPO, 2015. Zhong guo gu quan tou zi shi chang 2015 quan nian hui gu yu zhan shi [China VC/PE Market Review 2015]. Available at: http://wenku.baidu.com/link?url=bHN2fQ9GDqheMsDPD6Em7bNOH96nN5rreWT7LtXJvJfDLE-NdZlUAjdkKYlRXh25WY7UJKeSTdimfCsrU_3av2BmPqJxgarsafwjLHZ-Oz7. Accessed 12/10/2016 [in Chinese].

4

ECOSYSTEM ENTREPRENEURSHIP

Five cases of venturing in Alibaba's business ecosystem

4.1 Introduction

What happens inside a business ecosystem? Business ecosystems are widely characterized as dynamic systems of companies, products and technologies. However, what kind of innovation and business transformation do we see in a business ecosystem? Does an ecosystem support business diversification and disruption? In fact, Alibaba has made considerable efforts in keeping the business ecosystem entrepreneurial. For instance, in October 2014 Alibaba initiated a strategy called 'Baichuan Plan'. This plan offers mobile developers support to ensure that those developers with entrepreneurial ambition will get all kinds of resources from Alibaba once they are selected. So far 2,000 developers have been selected for the Baichuan Plan. The plan also includes a start-up competition with a prize of 5 million RMB seed fund for the best start-up. Lastly, the Baichuan Plan includes a Baichuan Entrepreneurship Base, which is currently located in Dream Town, Hangzhou. Besides the Baichuan Plan, Alibaba established an Innovation Centre in Suzhou in December 2016 together with a Chinese gaming company. The Innovation Centre is an incubation program for Internet entrepreneurs, cloud computing and big data ventures. Alibaba Cloud initiated a Maker Plus Platform in 2015, partnering with over 30 venture capital firms and 20 incubators and science parks. Every Maker will receive cloud computing resources and entrepreneurship education. Alibaba is keen on maintaining the entrepreneurial spirit.

In this chapter we analyze five cases of entrepreneurial venturing within Alibaba's business ecosystem. While the stories of AliHealth and Cainiao are exemplary for how new strategic nodes are created within Alibaba's business ecosystem based on opportunity recognition and intelligent opportunism, the stories of Koubei and Huashu illustrate the flexibility and willingness to experiment in the ecosystem. In addition to our research, see Section 1.4, the discussions with Li Zhiguo (former Koubei), Lu Liang (former Huashu), Chinese logistics professionals and domestic and foreign digital healthcare professionals and local entrepreneurs have been instrumental in developing the cases. The last case illustrates how Alibaba's business ecosystem has been a highly successful incubator for new ventures and a breeding ground for new CEOs.

4.2 Cross industry entrepreneurship: The story of AliHealth

"Alibaba wants to be in the health and happiness business. We will not build more hospitals, get more doctors or build more pharmaceutical factories. Instead, if we did the right thing, 30 years later, there will be fewer hospitals, pharmaceutical factories and doctors will be jobless."

—Ma Yun, Wuzhen World Internet Conference 2014
Note: free interpretation of the speech by the authors

In 2014, Alibaba took a controlling stake in CITIC 21 CN, a Hong Kong listed pharmaceutical information company, to breathe life in the vision of a healthy world of Ma Yun. The company was renamed AliHealth. This company was originally a Hong Kong registered company (established in 1971, originally a department store) and acquired by CITIC Group. In 2005 the company started a collaboration with China's National Food and Drug Administration to build a national drug electronic monitoring system. At the end of 2013 the company got the Chinese pilot license to sell pharmaceutical products online. Then, only two months later, Alibaba took a controlling stake in the company together with Ma Yun's Yunfeng Capital, reaching a 54% ownership.

In fact, this was not Alibaba's first move into the healthcare business. As an ecommerce focused platform, Tmall Pharmacy was established in 2012. While at that time Alibaba and Tmall did not have a license to sell medicine, the Tmall Pharmacy functioned mostly as a portal and would forward the user to external online pharmacies. In April of 2015, Tmall Pharmacy was merged into AliHealth through a 2.5 billion USD deal (Technode, 2015); therefore it eventually held the license for online medicine sales. However, in August 2016, the government stopped the experimental license for allowing online third party medicine sales. It made life difficult but not impossible for Alibaba's online medicine sales. Tmall Pharmacy changed the business process: once an order is placed, the shop will call the consumer and after confirmation send the medicine to the consumer. The payment is also done offline once the consumer receives the medicine. In this way, Alibaba circumvents the problem of no longer being allowed to sell medicine directly online.

AliHealth issued their vision via the Future Hospital Plan in May 2014. The ambition was to utilize Alipay's platform to enable users to register, monitor queues, conduct payments and review results as well as report on user experience. Currently there is a service window for each hospital that has a collaboration with Alibaba in the Alipay app. In the next phase the services will include insurance, reimbursements and settling accounts. In the long run, Alipay's Future Hospital also intends to collect all the medical data in the Alibaba Cloud and work together with wearable technology companies, medical institutions and even government to improve healthcare in China.

In December 2014 AliHealth launched an AliHealth app patient version. The App covers online consultation, registration, medicine purchase and drugstore searches among others. The app is in a way similar to other digital healthcare apps like Dr. Spring Rain, Guahaowang, Pingan Good Doctor; however, it seems to cover services more comprehensively. By the end of 2015, there are over two million downloads. The AliHealth App not only focuses on patients and users, but the 'hospital version' also focuses on small and medium sized medical institutions. In the 'hospital version', AliHealth aims to help these institutions to build a cloud based hospital information system, at the moment still for free.

Then, in March 2016, Alibaba took the next step in expanding its reach in the healthcare sector by investing in Wlycloud, a medical imaging data services company, with up to a 75% controlling stake for over 35 million USD. Founded in 2009, Wlycloud belonged to parent company Wandong Medical Equipment, one of the top medical imaging equipment manufacturers in China. Wylcloud's C2B and C2C services allow patients to upload their medical images in the AliHealth app and search for further professional opinions on the platform.

The experience of Alibaba in digital healthcare illustrates the fact that the regulatory environment is still under development with frequent changes and requires Alibaba to react creatively. In fact, innovation and regulation go hand in hand in China's digital healthcare market (Forbes, 2016). In a way, we see that AliHealth is co-evolving with its regulatory environment. Moreover, the market for digital healthcare in China is getting highly competitive with a wide variety of services and diverse players, from start-ups to large players such as Pingan and Alibaba. The digital healthcare in China is a highly fragmented but dynamic sector with both traditional and new players in the market. The story is not finished yet.

4.3 Cross industry entrepreneurship: The story of Cainiao smart logistics network

While talks of a smart logistics network initiative and open invitations for partners started publicly in January 2011, a new logistics company was only launched in May 2013, when Alibaba established a joint venture called *Cainiao*. The partners include China's top five largest private express delivery companies with a total investment of 300 billion RMB. Cainiao's goal is to create an intelligent platform for all relevant players like ecommerce, logistics, warehousing and other third party logistics service providers. Cainiao focuses on the main logistics planning, invests in warehouse construction strategically, and is fully open to all manufacturers, ecommerce companies and logistics providers. It is noteworthy that in December 2013 Alibaba also invested 280 million HKD in Haier Electronics, a Hong Kong listed subsidiary of Haier Group, and a large part of this investment (180 million HKD) went to RRS Logistics (in Chinese: *Ririshunwuliu*), a subsidiary of Haier Electronics which focuses on the household electronic appliances delivery, installation and service all over the country (Sina Tech, 2013). It is clear that Alibaba is committed to build a logistics capability and will not only bet on one horse.

The logic behind building a smart logistics networks is based on the limitations of the traditional ecommerce supply chain. In a traditional ecommerce supply chain, the commodity will be sent from the supplier's warehouse or distribution centre to the logistics provider's distribution centre, then go through various levels of the provider's logistics network until eventually arriving at the consumer's door. The chain is so long that it leads to low efficiency of the supply chain. At the same time, China's express delivery industry is still in the early growth stage. The main logistics service providers of ecommerce, like STO Express and YTO Express, are mostly following the franchise model; therefore the warehouse standards are not unified in different locations, the facilities are still of low level with manual sorting as the prior method. All in all, China's traditional ecommerce supply chain is facing a big challenge regarding distribution speed, efficiency and service quality.

Initially, Cainiao focused on building a warehouse network and purchased large numbers of land plots in cities like Tianjin, Shanghai, Guangzhou, Wuhan and Chengdu for warehouses. In 2013, the first warehouse in Tianjin started operating. By 2016, Cainiao had finished building a nationwide network of 150 warehouses. These warehouses are partly self-built while many are also from partners such as COSCO Logistics and EMS. Since Cainiao is a joint venture with China's largest express delivery companies, Cainiao is not only a warehousing infrastructure, it provides delivery services and solutions which are then executed by its express delivery partners. They also have value added services for other logistics suppliers, such as a standardized address database, both domestic and abroad; a big data driven system to aid delivery companies' mostly manual package sorting process; or, a benchmarking service for logistics companies to follow competitors' performance and service quality. Many of these services are data analytics services to improve efficiency and quality of delivery services. Since December 2015, Cainiao also offers cloud based enterprise resource planning (ERP) systems to logistics companies, where their full operating system can be integrated into Cainiao Cloud. So far, Yunda Express, Best Express, STO Express and TTK Express have already adopted Cainiao's cloud solutions.

In May 2014, Cainiao started online billing trial operations. Cainiao took the lead for the promotion of online billing with a uniform format, and provided this service for free to ecommerce and express companies. Cainiao provides technology solutions, system supports as well as reference prices, but does not participate in the process of bargaining between the merchants and the express companies. On the one hand, the use of online billing reduces the overall cost of the ecommerce value chain by optimizing the express delivery operation process. On the other hand, Cainiao can also strengthen its influence in the express delivery sector by promoting its own standards and billing systems. This will inevitably lead to more dependence of express delivery companies on Cainiao.

In May 2014 Cainiao announced its first external investment: KXTX (in Chinese: *Kaxingtianxia*). KXTX is a supply chain and logistics platform focusing on road transportation. It has logistic centres in 11 cities countrywide and claimed that more than 1,000 medium and small logistics companies have been integrated in its platform. Expanding quickly, in 2015 Cainiao announced that it had established the largest distribution centre supporting Tmall Supermarket sales in eastern China. The centre will enable next day delivery of groceries purchased online via Tmall Supermarket in 25 cities in Yangzi Delta area. In the same year, Cainiao started to build partnerships with local supermarkets, convenience stores and mom and pop stores to function as pick-up and delivery locations named Cainiao Post (in Chinese: *Cainiaoyizhan*), reaching over 40,000 local shops by the end of 2015. Attracting more flow to their local shops, shop owners are motivated to join Cainiao and even pay a small fee (~ 3,000 RMB) to become a member. By 2017, Cainiao processed the data over 70% of all packages in China, roughly 40 million packages per day.

Cainiao launched a cross border network service in September 2015, which included import and export logistics solutions. In order to get access to the global logistics supply chain, Alibaba cooperated with Singapore Post (July 2015), the US Postal Service (September 2015), the UK Royal Mail (October 2015) and Spanish Post (January 2016), and signed an agreement about Cainiao logistics construction with South Korea, implying its ambition of building an infrastructure for global trade and retail. In May 2016 Cainiao also announced their first-ever funding round from a consortium including Government of Singapore Investment Corp., Temasek Holdings and Khazanah Nasional Berha (Sovereign wealth fund of Malaysia). The presence of foreign investors in Cainiao once again suggests the company's ambition to expand overseas. Further expanding the cross border ecommerce logistics, Cainiao invested in 4PX (in Chinese: *Disifangsudi*), a cross border logistics service provider in July 2016 and established an alliance with Nippon Express to provide direct delivery for Japanese products purchased on Tmall International in August 2016.

By now, the Cainiao network covers 224 countries and regions but in a typical Alibaba way (distinguishing from Amazon), they do not own all the warehouses, planes and trucks, but work in partnerships. Cainiao uses partner warehouses in nine key countries, including the USA, the UK, Germany, Australia, Japan and South Korea, as consolidation centres where it helps gather parcels packages from the origin country and then ship them to China and global fulfilment centres in Hong Kong, Sydney and Melbourne.

Summarizing, Cainiao has three key features: intelligent cloud based systems, warehousing facilities and infrastructure and widespread partnerships. The latter not only refers to the joint venture partners but also new investments and global collaboration partners. With an endless ambition, Alibaba announced in 2016 that they will not only look abroad to expand, but have the vision also to expand domestically by building a rural logistics platform in collaboration with Alibaba's Rural Taobao program. Alibaba innovates logistics services in China by moving from reliance on external package delivery services, to creating a new ecosystem of logistics providers, merchants and clients. Although Cainiao is in itself a business ecosystem, it is interdependent with Alibaba's ecommerce platforms.

4.4 Spin-out: The story of Koubei

Li Zhiguo got his degree in English in 1996 and worked since 1998 as the manager of a foreign trade company. In 1998 he tried to start his own B2B business with classmates but failed. In 1999 he joined Alibaba as a young 22-year-old product manager, one of the first group of employees. In his after work hours, he started a house leasing website called eLeasing (in Chinese: *Yilinwang*). In 2004, he decided to quit Alibaba and worked full-time on his own venture: Koubei. At this time he is only 27 years old and full of ambition.

The name, Koubei, is appropriately chosen as it is part of an ancient Chinese proverb *koubeizaidao* that translates as 'all people everywhere are praising'. In this way the founder wants to benefit from the positive association with Chinese traditional culture. At the start, Koubei integrated the resources of eLeasing, which means it mostly focused on real estate information. However, at that time, the real estate market had not yet started to expand as it would a few years later. By 2005 the company won several awards and was generally considered a top 100 ecommerce platform in China. One year later, with only 30 employees, they received an investment from Alibaba. With the support of capital and user flow of Alibaba, Koubei became more ambitious. They no longer wanted to only focus on real estate information but started to include different aspects of local consumption and services, which is a similar aim as the currently successful local life service portals like 58.com. The founder however, was rather early with his venture and widely considered a pioneer. In 2006 Koubei was already industry leader and received a lot of media attention.

Witnessing the success of Dianping, the earliest restaurant review platform in China, and its large Google investment (4 million USD) in 2007, Li Zhiguo decided to change the strategic focus from a comprehensive local life service platform to only catering and restaurants. Within one year, Koubei included over 70,000 restaurants information, over two million daily unique users and over 200 employees. The promising growth indicated it was on the way to catch up with Dianping.

In 2008, Alibaba acquired Koubei and integrated Yahoo! China with Koubei initially. The idea of the merger was to boost both companies and make use of their respective advantages: at that time Yahoo! China still had a relatively good flow of users and reputation, while Koubei understood life service and had a strong execution capability. However, things did not work out as planned, as indicated by Mr. Li in an interview (Knowsky, 2014). The newly merged company faced difficulties in post merger integration. The company culture of Yahoo! China was mostly considered that of a large corporate, while Koubei's venture culture was suppressed right after they lost independence. This meant that a lot of the previous confidence and proactive attitude was limited in the merger. Besides, the merger also involved people from Taobao, who were considered to be more dominant. The integration issues made the collaboration unsuccessful from the start.

In 2009 Alibaba announced its Big Taobao Strategy and then Koubei was taken out of the Yahoo! China-Koubei merger and was integrated into Taobao. In 2009 Li Zhiguo left Koubei and moved to Ali Cloud; after he left, the business has had a series of leadership changes. At that time, the majority of the original Koubei employees already left the company. Li Zhiguo left Alibaba altogether in 2010 to established an angel investment fund focusing on Hangzhou based start-ups, investing in companies like Kuadi Taxi (later invested by Alibaba), Mogujie (fashion ecommerce) and Wacai (Internet financial services). In 2014 he became the CEO of Wacai. Although hopes were high for benefitting from Taobao's large user base, in fact, the number of Koubei's users went down. In addition, the gap with competitors Dianping and later Meituan was increasing rather than shrinking. By 2011, Alibaba stopped promoting Koubei and it slowly disappeared from the market. On an interesting note, even the domain name koubei.com.cn has expired.

The story of Koubei is a story of the Internet pioneer Li Zhiguo and the complex relations with Alibaba. Even though Koubei did not successfully rise to the top in Alibaba's ecosystem, there have been valuable, early lessons for Alibaba in how to incubate and later merge ventures into the ecosystem. But, as always in the story of Alibaba, this does not mean that the story is finished. In fact, Alibaba and Ant Financial have jointly reinitiated the brand of Koubei in 2015 to build an LBS platform. So far, the new company with the old brand name has already outcompeted industry leader Meituan Dianping with 15 million daily transactions and is currently the largest LBS platform in China (Trustdata, 2017).

4.5 Experimenting: The story of Huashu Taobao

The Chinese government announced in their tenth Five Year Plan (2001) that it planned to integrate the applications of the previously independent telecommunication, television and Internet networks, i.e. integration of three networks (in Chinese: *Sanwangronghe*). The aim was to have a multitude of functions and applications available in any of the three networks. The first real pilot plan only appeared in June 2010 with 12 cities as experimental locations. One of the challenges in such integration is the nature of the organizations involved in these three types of networks. Telecommunication networks are mostly run by state owned firms; television networks were until recently actually a public institution of government, while Internet has always been dominated by private firms, such as Alibaba.

As always, Alibaba is quick to jump into new opportunities and at the end of June 2010 Alibaba co-founded Huashu Taobao, a joint venture between Alibaba's Taobao (49%) and Huashu Media Network (51%), a fully state owned Hangzhou based cable TV operator, later to transform into a digital TV operator. The appointed CEO for Huashu Taobao was Lu Liang, a former R&D director in Taobao. During the launching ceremony Ma Yun said that operating a joint venture is difficult, but Alibaba will welcome such challenge.

The purpose of the joint venture was to integrate both companies' advantages and bridge Internet and digital television, to realize ecommerce on digital television and ecommerce of digital content. Ma Yun's ambition to occupy the television screen dates back to 2009. In 2009 Taobao partnered with Hunan TV and established a joint venture, called Happy Taobao. The aim was to use television programs to promote ecommerce and it is still running in 2017. With Huashu Taobao, the vision was further implemented by operating two platforms: Taohua Net and Huashu TV Taobao Mall. Taohua Net focused on selling digital content online, along the lines of Taobao's core business, with over 4,000 movies, 20,000 television episodes and over 1,000 entertainment shows uploaded right after launching the service. Huashu TV Taobao Mall focused on offering shopping service via digital television. Within the same year, Huashu TV Taobao Mall had over 100 shops participating with over 3,000 items. However, the daily sales averaged at around 100 items and the average spending was much less than on Taobao.

Unfortunately, it seems that Ma Yun's initial worry, the challenge of a joint venture, was prescient. First of all, even though Huashu Media can be considered a relatively market oriented state owned firm, they lacked the commitment and commercial spirit. This shows in the fact that the employees of the joint venture were mostly from Taobao, rather than Huashu Media. Second, the sales of Huashu TV Taobao Mall were disappointing from the first moment. Taobao appeared unable to channel its huge user base to the digital content ecommerce platform. Third, the employees of Huashu Taobao understood ecommerce very well; however, they were not familiar enough with the TV world, which was exactly the shift of attention that Taobao was looking for. As the CEO Lu Liang said, the experience and tools for promotion online seemed not to work well in the TV world (Alicloud Consulting, 2014). So, they ended up using traditional promotion tools such as direct mail and banners. It was a lesson that this target market was really different from the usual netizens.

Considering the lack of success, Alibaba decided by the end of 2011 to merge Huashu Taobao into Taobao. However, this did not mean that the initiative stopped completely. In September 2013, Alibaba started selling the Huashu Rainbow, a set top box developed by Huashu Media that allows users to connect their TV to the Internet (Technode, 2013). Moreover, in 2014 Ma Yun together with Shi Yuzhu, a well known Chinese investor, invested 6.5 billion RMB into Huashu Media and meanwhile Alibaba also formed a strategic partnership with Huashu Media. It seems the story is not finished yet.

4.6 Ali incubator: The story of hundreds of new CEOs

Huashu Taobao's Lu Liang and Koubei's Li Zhiguo have in common that they both incubated ventures within Alibaba's ecosystem. While the majority of Chinese entrepreneurs are grassroots entrepreneurs, i.e. starting from zero, a fair amount of entrepreneurs in the Internet business spin out from the large technology companies in China. Equipped with knowledge, experience and in particular networks, these entrepreneurs tend to have higher success rates. In fact, most Internet entrepreneurs that have corporate experience come from just a dozen domestic and foreign technology companies: Baidu, Alibaba, Tencent, Microsoft, Google, Yahoo!, Huawei, IBM, Shanda, Kingsoft, Sohu, Netease and Sina. These technology companies play a significant role as incubator and investor in new Internet companies. Alibaba has been, by far, the most active generator of new CEOs. By the beginning of 2016, already over 450 individuals came out of Alibaba to start their ventures. In total over 250 ventures have been established by previous Alibaba employees (Huxiu, 2016). Please see Table 4.1 for several representative ventures.

The ventures founded by former Alibaba employees include many different types of business and are in different investment phases, from early stage to pre-IPO, usually just a few years after establishment. For instance, one interesting company was established by Chen Lian in 2015. The venture received an A round investment and focused on helping companies to identify and claim violations of copyrights. Basically a client outsources the search for violations of their online content to his venture, called Right Knights, and they receive the claim reimbursement if they successfully file the copyright violation claim. Another former employee started a venture which is riding the waves of sustainability and environmental protection. Tan Biao established his venture 9beike in 2015 as well and focused on developing

TABLE 4.1 Representative ventures established by former Alibaba employees

Venture	(Co) Founder	Investment phase	Investment size of latest phase	Business
Right Knights (2015)	Chen Lian	A round	10 million RMB	Copyright monitoring service
9beike (2015)	Tan Biao	A round	NA	Secondhand collection
Tongdun Technology (2013)	Jiang Tao	B round	30 million USD	Big data security
Treebear Network (2012)	Lai Jie	B round	200 million RMB	B2B WiFi service
Mogujie (2010)	Chen Qi	D round	200 million USD	Mobile social ecommerce
Tongcheng Travel (LY.com) (2004)	Wu Zhixiang	D round	6 billion RMB	Online travel agent
Xiami Music (2006)	Wang Hao	Alibaba acquired	15 million USD	Music platform

an app that allows users to put their secondhand stuff online and let it be collected by 9beike. The venture will then either recycle or resell, more or less replacing the informal recycling individuals that haunt many residential areas in China. Since they are still in early stage of his venture, their operating model is not yet clear, but promising.

Besides the early stage ventures, a venture like Tongdun Technology established by Jiang Tao in 2013 just received 30 million USD. This company focuses on utilizing big data analytics to do risk assessment of online fraud, such as transactions and accounts. Another example is a venture that got direct investment from Alipay and received B round investment of 200 million RMB from an external investor: Treebear Network. This venture, established in 2013 by Lai Jie, focused on developing B2B WiFi solutions and closely collaborated with Alipay on their offline shops expansion. Some of these ventures have become very successful – for instance, Mogujie, founded by Chen Qi, former Zhejiang University student, in 2010. The company is in mobile social ecommerce for young lady fashion. It also claims to play an advising role in fashion selection as to distinguish from the other fashion ecommerce platforms. It recently is preparing to go public and it appears the investment world sees the value considering the latest D round of 200 million USD. A couple of months later, early 2016, the company merged with the similar competitor Meilishuo. Critics may claim this to be an exception; however, Alibaba's ecosystem in recently years has given rise to another unicorn: Tongcheng Travel. This company's founder, Wu Zhixiang, left Alibaba in the early days, 2002, similar to Koubei's Li Zhiguo. There are also more stories like Koubei. In 2006, Wang Hao established Xiami Music, an online music platform, not unlike Spotify but without the paid subscription model. Xiami Music was acquired by Alibaba in 2013.

According to research (Hexun, 2011) the majority of ventures spun out of Alibaba are in the ecommerce sector, over 30%. Except ecommerce there are ventures in travelling, financial services, enterprise services, social network services, software tool and lastly electronic hardware. Over 40% got investment, as compared to an Internet industry average of >20% in China, and half of these are A round venture capital investments and over 30% is still in angel investment phase. Around 10% of these spin-outs have already gotten to the B round investment stage. While some of these investments come from Alibaba, like in the case of Koubei and Treebear, the majority are external investors. Also, sometimes entrepreneurs that come out of the Alibaba ecosystem received investments from Alibaba's competitors (like Tencent), like in the case of Didi Chuxing, currently the most successful taxi hailing app in China, established by a former Alibaba employee Cheng Wei. In fact, Alibaba invested in Didi Chuxing's competitor Kuaidi, founded by Chen Weixing, who was not previously part of the Alibaba ecosystem. These are signals of a healthy and dynamic ecosystem, where the boundaries of the ecosystem are fluid and open.

4.7 Insights: Cross industry innovation and ecosystem entrepreneurship

In this chapter we distinguish four types of ecosystem entrepreneurial transformations that are facilitated in Alibaba's ecosystem: 1) cross industry innovation; 2) spin-out; 3) experimentation; 4) incubating new ventures. In particular cross industry innovation is an advantage of business ecosystems as illustrated by the entry of Alibaba into digital healthcare with the story of AliHealth and the disruptive move into logistics with the story of Cainiao. Moreover, as seen in Sections 4.4–4.6, Alibaba's ecosystem is facilitating entrepreneurship. It is important to highlight the success of Alibaba's business ecosystem as an incubator for new CEOs and ventures in a wide variety of sectors (see Section 4.6). Table 4.2 summarizes our cases, the diversification strategy they represent and the outcomes. None of these stories is 'finished' but, typical for business in China, developing and changing, as illustrated by the renewed Koubei brand together with its successful new LBS business. And that is exactly what is possible inside Alibaba's ecosystem: room for experimentation and failure besides boosting successes.

According to classic strategic management, one strategy for growth is expanding by strategic entrepreneurship. Taking a business ecosystem as a unit of analysis, we can conclude that a business ecosystem is highly facilitative of entrepreneurial activities, both within, across and outside of the ecosystem. Moreover, given the high success of business incubation and the 'graduation' of hundreds of new CEOs, we posit that the growth of Alibaba's business ecosystem is partly explained by *ecosystem entrepreneurship*, in contrast to planned strategic entrepreneurship.

TABLE 4.2 Cases of ecosystem entrepreneurship

Case	Diversification strategy	Outcome
AliHealth	cross industry innovation	New strategic node
Cainiao	cross industry innovation	New strategic node
Koubei	spin-out	Merged into existing company Taobao and later the brand is used for new LBS business
Huashu Taobao	experimentation	Merged into existing company Taobao
Hundreds of new CEOs	incubation and spin-out	Exit out of the ecosystem, 40% of the ventures successfully raised capital

References

Alicloud Consulting, 2014. Hua shu tao bao xin hun fan nao: mei tian xiao liang pai huai zai 100 duo dan [Huashu Taobao newlywed headache: Daily sales linger around 100 orders]. Available at: https://www.aliyun.com/zixun/content/2_6_177914.html?spm=5176.100033.400001.14.WEiRGP. Accessed 10/02/2017 [in Chinese].

Forbes, 2016. Balancing act: China's online healthcare system needs both innovation and regulation. Available at: https://www.forbes.com/sites/benjaminshobert/2016/11/29/the-incredible-potential-and-challenges-facing-chinas-online-healthcare-system/#480a849c3c99. Accessed 30/12/2016.

Hexun, 2011. Zhi fu bao kuai jie zhi fu yong hu nian di you wang po 4000 wan [Alipay users may reach over 40 million by the end of this year]. Available at: http://www.ebrun.com/20111027/34796.shtml. Accessed 10/02/2017 [in Chinese].

Huxiu, 2016. Zhong guo hu liang wang chuang ye pai xi pan dian zhi a li ba ba xi [Chinese Internet entrepreneurs inventory of Alibaba]. Available at: https://www.huxiu.com/article/139034/1.html?f=index_feed_article. Accessed 10/02/2017 [in Chinese].

Knowsky, 2014. Zhuan fang li zhi guo: qian a li b aba di 46 hao yuan gong [Interview with Li Zhiguo: Former Alibaba employee number 46]. Available at: http://www.knowsky.com/578194.html. Accessed 10/02/2017 [in Chinese].

Sina Tech, 2013. A li b aba 22 yi yuan tou zi hai er, kuo zhan da jian shang pinwu liu [Alibaba invests 2.2 billion RMB in Haier, expanding large product logistics]. Available at: http://tech.sina.com.cn/i/2013-12-09/08238987877.shtml. Accessed 10/02/2017 [in Chinese].

Technode, 2015. Alibaba injects Tmall's online pharmacy business into Alibaba Health. Available at: http://technode.com/2015/04/15/alibaba-health/. Accessed 10/02/2017.

Technode, 2013. Hands on first STB powered by Alibaba Smart TV OS, Wasu Rainbow. Available at: http://technode.com/2013/09/16/hands-on-first-stb-powered-by-alibaba-smart-tv-os-wasu-rainbow/. Accessed 10/02/2017.

Trustdata, 2017. 2016 Nian ben di sheng huo fu wu O2O bai pi shu [Whitepaper of the 2016 local life services O2O]. Available at: http://mt.sohu.com/20170208/n480172485.shtml. Accessed 10/02/2017 [in Chinese].

5

CONTINUOUS INNOVATION

Ant Financial pioneering Internet finance (Chinese FinTech)

5.1 Introduction

Alibaba has a long track record of innovations: from commercializing the first online trading platform, to pioneering online third party payment, but also organizing the business in a novel way, i.e. business ecosystem, and developing a business process that facilitates high levels of new venture creation unlike traditional companies. In order to better understand how Alibaba's business ecosystem has developed and grown, we take one example of continuous innovation: Ant Financial. In fact, Ant Financial has only existed for three years but is the amalgamation of Alibaba's innovation efforts in financial technology over the last decade. Financial technology (FinTech) is an emerging global industry that uses new digital technology to replace or enhance financial services of incumbent organizations. In China business professionals refer to Internet finance rather than FinTech due to translation issues (in Chinese: huliangwangjinrong). In the remainder of the book we will refer to Internet finance.

The push into Internet finance opens up a new means of financing other than resorting to the capital market or conventional banks. In the era of big data, Internet finance has the potential to upend the market, profit and survival models of traditional financial institutions (Financial Times, 2017a). Big data incorporates all sorts of information on a platform accessible to many people. The chance of a company defaulting on its loans can be more easily calculated by looking at the data of its past performance instead of only looking at its balance sheet. Internet and mobile technology in combination with big data reduces information asymmetry and Alibaba is well positioned as one of the largest repositories of consumer and business data.

After pioneering China's first online third party payment service Alipay, Alibaba expanded into the Internet financial services sector with products like Ali Loan, Zhongan Insurance and Ant Financial. Other Internet companies quickly joined the competition including Tencent, Baidu, Xiaomi, LeEco and Alibaba's ecommerce competitor JD. To survive and stay competitive, these companies must keep innovating their products. Internet finance in China is like the" "Wild East" with many new entrants and relatively few rules and regulations.

While the government has encouraged financial reforms and opening up markets, it has been uneasy with the rapid developments of online financial services and faced difficulty in catching up. As we will see in the case of Ant Financial, the regulatory environment has been trying to monitor, if not control, the development in Internet finance. While sometimes being lenient, as in the case of allowing Alipay's experiment with third party online payments for six years relatively unregulated and approving online banking licenses in 2014, at other times the market is more strictly controlled such as in personal lending and SME loans.

In this chapter, we explore innovation as a growth strategy for a business ecosystem by discussing the Ant Financial case. This chapter is an extension of the research in Greeven et al. (2016) and based on extensive evidence of Chinese financial newspapers and industry reports in addition to the empirical research as described in Section 1.4. We start by discussing the need for online financial services and then describe how Alibaba developed a series of innovative services and products. Then, we explore the challenges of this newly emerging business, in particular in terms of operations and changing regulations. Overall, these innovations allowed Alibaba's business ecosystem to expand and diversify.

5.2 The need for Internet finance

The financial sector in China is one of the most heavily regulated industries with a high threshold and strong monopolization. The establishment of the market mechanism of the financial sector in China has been slow. The purpose of the high threshold was to guarantee the financial security and protect consumers, but it also resulted in higher profit margins for the mostly state owned financial industry than any other industries. The financial products and services supply for the private sector and individuals in China was in shortage.

5.2.1 Needs of SMEs

The development of SMEs in China is closely connected with the development of the whole Chinese economy. SMEs in China make up the majority of all enterprises and represent close to 70% of total GDP by 2016 (China Statistical Yearbook, 2016). However, most SMEs could not use direct financing such as stock financing and bond financing due to the regulatory constraints. Meanwhile, due to relatively low credibility of SMEs, higher managing costs for small size loans as well as the inertia of banks, it was also not easy for SMEs to get loans from banks. For instance, a mere 0.4% of state bank credit reached private business in 1998 and according to the 2003 World Bank Investment Climate Survey for China, SMEs in China obtain only 12% of their working capital from bank loans in 2002. Therefore, private loans, underground financing and illegal lending and financing networks have been common and form a large part of the business sector in China. Credit cooperatives, especially in the coastal entrepreneurial regions of China, have bloomed. Even when officially prohibited, local governments in, for instance, Fujian and Zhejiang have generally tolerated alternative private finance mechanisms. With the rise of the Internet and associated efficiency and anonymity, such approaches prospered. Nevertheless, considering the high risk and overall undersupply, the demand of many SMEs and individual financial consuming services could not be satisfied. There is still an estimated financing need of 17 trillion RMB for SMEs in China in 2013 (Qianzhan, 2013), the moment when the window of opportunity for Internet finance further opened.

5.2.2 Needs of individuals

Owing to past strict investment restrictions and lack of professional services by the state owned banks, in particular for the lower middle class, individuals in China had limited means to manage their wealth and saving was by far the most common way. Moreover, many of the 600 million farmers in China did not know anything about wealth management, while the denomination 'farmer' is not equal to lack of savings and capital. The saving rate per capita in China was close to three times that of the USA and it increased to 46% in 2016 (The World Fact Book, 2016). It ranked the third globally in 2016, right after Surinam and Singapore. However, deposit rates has been unattractive and deliberately fixed and controlled by the state. In 2015, the People's Bank of China still reduced the benchmark deposit rate five times.

5.2.3 Needs for a better credit system

In 2016, the credit system of the People's Bank of China covered approximately 880 million people, or 64% of the whole population, significantly improved after the effort of the Chinese government (the cover rate was only 24% in 2013). This is still less than the cover rate of 85% in the USA (Csai News, 2015). Moreover, China's credit system is not comprehensive which means most of the credit related information is still isolated or incomplete. With the development of online credit, the credit system will cover a larger group of people while providing more relevant information. The data gathered from the Internet can enable online credit to reach into daily life scenes, like car renting or hotel booking. In 2015, the People's Bank of China issued license for individual credit to eight companies for the first time in the history, including not only traditional credit firms but also Internet giants like Alibaba and Tencent.

5.2.4 Needs for financial reform: The 2013 window of opportunity

The year 2013 was an important year of financial reform in China. The guiding principle of the reform was to loosen regulation but enhance supervision.

The former was to provide the market with discretion, while the latter aimed to enhance legitimacy of the process and supervision. The financial reform aimed to gradually enable maturity and diversification of capital markets, lower industry threshold to facilitate a freer market, enable a market based pricing mechanism and further develop asset securitization. As one of the consequences, the profit of traditional financial institutions earned by beneficial policies would decline, while private and emerging forces like Internet finance companies will gain reform dividends. A window of opportunity opened up further for Internet finance in China.

5.3 Innovations in Internet finance

Alibaba brought several innovations to the Chinese financial services sector. Table 5.1 summarizes Alibaba's key innovations in the field of Internet financial services from 2002-2014. They will be discussed in more detail later.

5.3.1 Chengxintong: First online credit system

Around the 2000s, most of China's emerging SMEs were not covered in a credit rating system. However, the development of B2B online business demanded a credit system to allow mutual trust between vendors in a transaction. In order to promote B2B ecommerce, in 2002 Alibaba established Chengxintong as a credit rating system on her domestic B2B platform 1688.com. This credit system uses third party certification, activity records, member ratings and other credentials to comprehensively evaluate the vendor. A report from Alibaba indicated that 92% of their vendors would select transaction partners based on the information of this system (Peking University Business Review, 2007). The development and launch of this comprehensive system was the first in China and significantly improved the business ecosystem for ecommerce at an early stage of its development. By 2016, it has certified over one million SMEs with more than 30 million SMEs using the system to facilitate their business (Tencent Finance, 2016).

TABLE 5.1 Alibaba's Internet finance innovations

Year	Product	Innovations
2002	Chengxintong	First online credit system
2004	Alipay	Revolutionizing online payment
2007, 2010, 2014	AliLoan	Challenging SME loans
2013	Zhongan Insurance	First Internet insurance company
2013	Yu'ebao	Pioneering online wealth management
2014	Ant Financial	Integrating online financial services

5.3.2 Alipay: Revolutionizing online payment

At the end of 2004, Alibaba launched her online payment service Alipay. At that time, online credit cards or debit card payments were rare in China and customers usually paid cash in their everyday life. By providing an escrow payment service, Alipay reduced transaction risk for online consumers: after the buyer placed an order, he or she needed to pay directly to an escrow account; later, when the buyer received the goods and was satisfied, he or she can confirm the deal being completed, then the payment will be transferred from the escrow account to the seller. Clearly, this innovative product creates the necessary safeguard that both Chinese online buyers and sellers need. By 2006, Alipay had already formed partnerships with over 40 major Chinese banks and signed a long term strategic agreement with China Post so customers could fund their Alipay account at any of China Post's 66,000 locations across the country without a debit or a bank card. This agreement helped Alibaba and Taobao penetrate China's underdeveloped regions, where post office money remittance and parcel delivery were more common than bank and courier services (Jinghua Times, 2006).

In 2007, Alipay launched an online payment service to help merchants worldwide sell directly to consumers in China, cooperating with over 300 global retail brands and supporting transactions in 12 major foreign currencies. With its new international transaction service, Alibaba could also further penetrate overseas markets. In fact, Alipay still had not received any formal recognition from the government nor a specific license, while already operating abroad. In May 2011, Alipay eventually obtained the license to operate third party payment business from the People's Bank of China, after more than six years' experimental operations. This is not unusual in China and we have seen many examples where regulation is following technology and market, quietly allowing certain experiments without government approval or explicit disapproval.

The number of Alipay users increased sharply. By 2014 the number of real name registration with Alipay reached approximately 300 million (Zhang, 2014) and by June 2016, its monthly active users reached about 300 million as well (see Figure 5.1). Alipay has a dominant market share compared with other main third party payment companies such as Tencent's Tenpay and state owned Unionpay (see Figure 5.2). Moreover, mobile payments in China are far more accepted by Chinese consumers than American consumers, an advantage perhaps of leapfrogging directly to mobile digital payment (Financial Times, 2017b).

Alipay is no longer a payment service but stretched out to connect the other businesses of Alibaba to create an ecosystem. Alipay has become a crucial glue in the large business ecosystem. Nowadays, when a user turned on his or her Alipay app on the mobile, the user can easily connect with location based services to book a taxi, movie tickets, order take-out food, and find the nearest gas station. To repay the credit card, top up the mobile phone, pay the electricity or gas bill and book train tickets, users only need to open the Alipay app. Moreover, in addition to direct access to Alibaba's ecommerce platforms Taobao and Tmall,

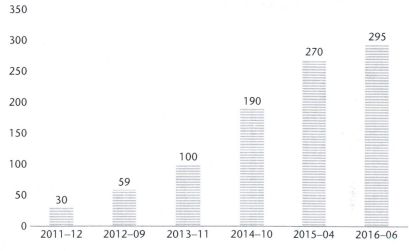

FIGURE 5.1 Alipay monthly active users (in millions)

Source: Compiled year by year from Hexun [2011], CNNIC [2012], Alipay [2013], Netease [2014], Sina [2015], Analysys [2016].

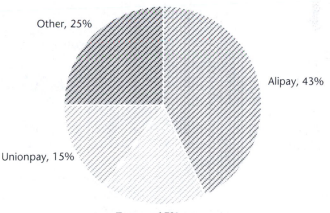

FIGURE 5.2 Market share of third party payments in China (2016, Q2)

Source: DATA adopted from Analysys [2016].

Alipay offered Huabei, an online consumer loan that allows installment payments to purchase on Taobao and Tmall. Users can also manage money saved in Alipay to buy the monetary market fund Yu'ebao or other wealth management products in Ant Financial.

5.3.3 AliLoan: Challenging SME loans

One particular challenge for SMEs in China is access to bank loans. In order to further facilitate SMEs to adopt Alibaba's platforms and expand their business, Alibaba has initiated SME loans. However, it has proven to be a big challenge and Alibaba has continuously experimented and innovated its products in partnership with key institutional stakeholders. First, in 2007, Alibaba partnered with the China Construction Bank and the Industrial and Commercial Bank of China, China's largest commercial banks, to provide members with online, jointly vouched loans. It connected three or more SMEs as a union to request loans from banks without any collateral and the joint SMEs would bear risk together. Alibaba provided banks with credit records of its members; banks provided loans and were responsible for risk control. However, this partnership ceased in 2010. The fact that large banks were unfamiliar with SMEs' risk profile and behaviour has increased the cost in the risk evaluation and control, and also limited the outcomes for the banks. The failure of the cross-guarantee collateral free loan indicated that banks could not meet the needs of SMEs; therefore Alibaba decided to establish its own lending company.

In June 2010, Alibaba established Zhejiang Ali Small Loan Company with a license issued by Zhejiang Provincial Administration for Industry & Commerce. One year later, Alibaba established Chongqing Ali Small Loan Company. These two loan companies provided clients with loans of less than 500,000 RMB (Caijing, 2014). However, due to financial restriction, Alibaba could only fund its lending business from its own pocket. Then, in 2014, Alibaba partnered with seven Chinese banks to offer unsecured business loans to small exporters. Under the new initiative, small businesses that participated in Alibaba's OneTouch trade services platform could borrow from 1 million RMB up to 10 million RMB depending on their recent overseas sales histories and credit worthiness (Alizila, 2014).

As the most recent and big step in innovating SME loans, Ant Financial together with several other partners established MYbank and received a private bank license issued by China Banking Regulatory Commission and started to operate in June 2015. By the end of 2016, there were a total of 16 licenses issued to non-traditional (often Internet driven) companies. MYbank focuses on offering financial services for consumers, farmers and SMEs, in particular SMEs in the ecommerce sector. Loan applicants can directly log into MYbank with their Alipay, Taobao, 1688 or Aliexpress accounts and they can get credit loans with variable interest rates based on their credit evaluation which includes information available in Alibaba's various platforms as well as relevant information from other partners, such as CNZZ, a web traffic statistics institution. The maximum amount can be 1 million RMB. By the end of 2016, MYbank had served over 800,000 SMEs with a total loan amount of over 45 billion RMB. Altogether Alibaba has developed (but also failed) several innovative SME loan products with relentless effort, until eventually they can run their own SME focused bank.

5.3.4 Zhongan insurance: First online insurance company

In response to consumer needs, in November 2013, Alibaba partnered with Tencent and Ping An Insurance to establish China's first online insurance company, Zhongan Insurance, with a license granted by China Insurance Regulatory Commission. The premium scale of Zhongan insurance was small after its launch in 2014 but witnessed a sharp increase in 2015; it obtained a 2.3 billion RMB premium with a nearly 200% annual growth rate (Sohu, 2016). Moreover, in 2015, Zhongan raised an A round funding of 900 million USD with a surprisingly high market valuation of 8 billion USD (Startup-Partner, 2015). So far, Zhongan has already launched over 300 insurance products, some of which are widely considered to be star products and quite innovative. For instance, Bububao is a health insurance which connects consumers' smart wearable step counting to their insurance premium; i.e. the more they walk, the less they need to pay (China Finance and Economy Times, 2017). Another offbeat insurance is coverage for alcohol poisoning while watching football (Financial Times, 2016).

5.3.5 Yu'ebao: Pioneering online wealth management

In 2013, Alipay had attracted around 100 million users with real name registration (Alipay, 2013) but Alibaba could not provide users who deposited their money in Alipay account with an interest like commercial banks. With the increasing need for individual wealth management and the ceiling of bank deposit interest rates, Alibaba launched a product named Yu'ebao that allowed its users to invest money deposited in Alipay into a monetary market fund managed by Tian Hong Asset Management. It is important to note that Yu'ebao is different from the other monetary market funds in the market. It can be used directly or withdrawn immediately whenever needed while the other funds have a one day delay in retrieval. The fund offered an annual return of around 3.6%, which was very attractive considering the fixed 0.35% interest offered on typical commercial bank deposits (Financial Times, 2013). It attracted 230,000 users within three days and by September 2014, the assets reached 55.7 billion RMB. Yu'ebao became the largest monetary market fund in China only one year after its launch (Alizila, 2013) (see Figure 5.3). Followed by Alibaba's Yu'ebao, Baidu, JD, Tencent and other Internet companies as well as commercial banks also collaborated with fund management companies to sell monetary market funds online. By 2015 there were about a dozen Internet companies and 20 banks selling monetary market funds after the initial success of Yu'ebao.

5.3.6 Ant Financial: Integrating online financial services

In October 2014, Alibaba established *Ant Financial*, the former Ali Xiaowei Finance Service Group, a comprehensive financial services company positioning itself as inclusive finance to serve individuals and SMEs. Ma Yun and roughly 25 of the co-founders or early employees of Alibaba hold 76% of Ant Financial's shares.

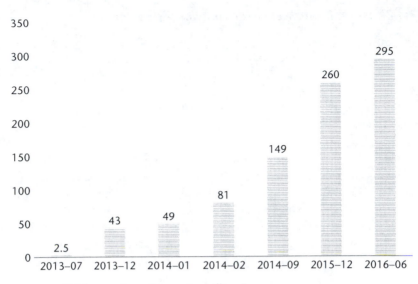

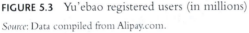

FIGURE 5.3 Yu'ebao registered users (in millions)

Source: Data compiled from Alipay.com.

Currently, Alibaba does not directly own shares of Ant Financial, only indirectly via their co-founders ownership. Alipay and Yu'ebao are both part of Ant Financial. Ant Financial has brought to market many new financial products such as Huabei for online consumer loans, Ant Dake for Crowdfunding, Ant Fortune for wealth management, and Ant Financial Cloud for cloud services for financial institutions. Ant Financial and affiliated Alipay have been active investors both domestically and in nearby Asian markets such as India, South Korea, Thailand and the Philippines, as illustrated in Section 3.3 and Chapter 6. An overview of Ant Finance's products and services is shown in Table 5.2.

In the years following the establishment of Ant Financial, several important events mark the maturing of Ant Financial and the new Internet financial sub-ecosystem inside Alibaba's business ecosystem. In May 2015, Zhejiang Banking Regulatory Commission granted Alibaba an Internet banking license. MyBank, owned by Ant Financial Group and a couple of other companies, held one of six new banking licenses granted to privately owned companies under a pilot scheme aimed at diversifying China's financial system. In March 2015, Alibaba and the world's biggest peer-to-peer (P2P) lending platform, Lending Club, formed a partnership. On Lending Club's platform, the US customers could get small business loans from Alibaba (Financial Times, 2015). A move to enter the international online financial markets and deeper globalization of Alibaba's business ecosystem. In July 2015, Ant Financial received A round funding from eight investment institutions such as China's National Social Insurance Fund, CDB Capital, with a super unicorn valuation of 45 billion USD and in April 2016, Ant Financial raised 4.5 billion USD with an even larger evaluation of 60 billion USD. Given its current valuation and prospects, an historic IPO is expected.

TABLE 5.2 Ant Financial products (2016)

Product name	Introduction
Alipay	Third party payment
Yu'ebao	Current financial product for individuals
Zhaocaibao	Regular financial product for individuals
Ant Fortune	One stop wealth management platform for individuals
Zhima Fortune	Individual credit system
Huabei	Online consumer loan
Alipay	Third party payment
Ants Daq	Crowdfunding platform
Ant Financial Cloud	Cloud service for financial institutions
MYbank	Internet bank

5.4 Challenges: Regulation and business

5.4.1 Dynamic regulatory environment: Clarifications and challenges

Two specific regulations and guidelines in 2015 are of particular interest as they influenced the Internet finance sector significantly. First, on July 2015, ten central government ministries and industry regulators jointly released guidelines related to the governance of the Internet finance sector. The guidelines clarified the definition of Internet finance and the responsibility of each supervising organization regarding different types of business. The guideline further specified directions and regulations on certain business types. Crowdfunding should serve small and micro sized enterprises and start-ups. In terms of P2P, the guideline made it clear that it was under the constraint of Contract Law of PRC, General Principles of the Civil Law of PRC and other related laws. It should be positioned as intermediary of information rather than intermediary of credit, which means P2P could only promote transaction but should not connect with funds of investors, attract funds or deposits or lend loans.

Second, on July 31, 2015, the Peoples' Bank of China released a draft of regulations on non-bank payment companies. It set tighter regulation on the verifying process of transactions and regulated the accumulated payment amount of an individual client. Furthermore, it inhibited such payment companies to open accounts for companies that involved business on loan, financing, wealth management or money exchange. Companies in such businesses should open accounts at commercial banks. This regulation would mostly affect third party payment companies. Derivatives of these companies would be restricted and companies had to return to their basic payment business. Large payment companies might well survive in the stricter regulation due to scale effect and partnership with banks, while small payment companies with fewer resources might be forced out of the market. In May 2011, the People's Bank of China issues 27 licenses to third party payment companies. Until May 2015, there have been over 250 third party payment companies. In another further restriction policy, on August 6, 2015, the Supreme People's Court unveiled regulation on private lending, setting 35% as the cap private loan's annual interest. This might hinder some online loan products, in particular those that attract clients with high interest. Altogether, the new regulations have provided clarifications on Internet finance and in particular the governance mechanisms. At the same time, the new regulations also hinder some of the Internet finance business models.

5.4.2 Business challenges

Challenges for Internet financial service providers are not just regulatory. These companies have to carefully monitor Internet fraud, which is still the number one risk with online payment in China. They also have to be careful with financial risks inherent in their products. Small sized investors and lenders were especially sensitive to losses. However, the first challenge for Ant Financial is limited source of funds which constraints its lending capability. Since it is forbidden to absorb public deposits, Alibaba can only use its own equity funds to provide loans or get a financing fund from banks with a certain leverage ratio. The second challenge is about product innovation. While competition keeps growing, Alibaba finds the speed of its innovation slowing down. For instance, Ant Finance's key product Yu'ebao was no longer unique soon after its launch in the market, nor highly profitable. Third, risk control and trust is always a concern. For instance, Zhaocaibao facilitated their users to buy private bonds of Qiaoxing Group. In their general promotion they guaranteed a stable return on their products. However, Qiaoxing Group defaulted on their bonds, a total of 300 million RMB, and did not pay back the users on time (TechWeb, 2016). This product had an insurance policy, underwritten by a local bank. Nevertheless, the bank said that the insurance guarantee letter was fake. The value of the bonds has not yet fully been paid back to the users and the negotiations are ongoing. Clearly, this has signalled the market that buying financial products on Zhaocaibao is not reliable. Lastly, Internet security is a serious risk for online payment. Cyber criminals can decipher Alipay users' payment codes or use forged websites to cheat on users. Altogether despite its significant success, we still see a lot of business challenges for Ant Financial in addition to the regulatory dynamics.

5.5 Insights: Continuous innovation across industry boundaries

In this chapter we use Ant Financial as an example to illustrate how Alibaba's business ecosystem is continuously innovating. Alibaba has successfully opened up a new market in China: Internet finance (FinTech). Ant Financial has developed into a strategic node within Alibaba's business ecosystem by continuous cross industry innovation. Why did Alibaba develop innovations in the Internet finance field? The market opportunity, with the needs of SMEs and individuals, was clearly there and at the same time the current credit system was insufficient and left an institutional gap. In combination with financial reforms in 2013 that allowed maturing and diversification of the capital markets, there was a vacuum waiting to be filled by a newcomer. Alibaba was well positioned with the wide acceptance of Alipay and a new growth model of diversification. However, the opportunities in the market and the supporting regulatory environment were not the only drivers; in fact, the increasing competition from other Internet companies and incumbents of the finance industry also necessitated Alibaba's continuous innovation.

While online financial services are seemingly far from the core business of Alibaba, a closer look at the motivation of cross industry innovation reveals clear synergies and complementarities. First, Internet companies like Alibaba have enormous online traffic, i.e. online channel resources. They are selling diverse offerings to the significant user pool. For example, Yu'ebao as an innovative offering is essentially selling a monetary fund online. It is not closely related to the original business, but it can increase the revenue by making better use of the existent channel resources. Second, some financial offerings are directly related to the original business scenario; therefore they can reinforce or improve the original business. For example, Huabei, a mini consumption loan, can encourage the consumers to spend more on Alibaba's ecommerce platforms. Third, some financial offerings, such as the SME credit system Chengxintong and the personal credit system Zhima Credit, function as the foundation for a lot of other businesses in the ecosystem, creating synergies. Table 5.3 summarizes how external and internal drivers fuel Alibaba's continuous innovation.

Innovation does not refer to new product development or breakthrough technologies by research and development alone. It refers to developing new products, new ways to organize the production processes; opening up new markets, new technologies and new business models, as ways to grow the company's business. Alibaba developed six crucial innovations in Internet finance that were not only a pioneering credit system, online payment, SME loans, online insurance and wealth management but also developed a comprehensive and integrated

TABLE 5.3 External and internal drivers for Alibaba's continuous innovation

External drivers		Internal drivers
Market opportunity		Synergy with other businesses
Dynamic regulatory environment	**Continuous innovation**	
Fierce competition		Exploiting current resources
Institutional gap		

Internet finance ecosystem. Alibaba's Internet finance innovations also include business model innovations. For example, the several different experiments with ways to provide the much needed loans to SMEs are perhaps not driven by technology but by business model changes. Online insurance includes both new products and also combinations of existing products.

By now, Ant Financial is an ecosystem in itself, although still strongly connected to Alibaba's core platforms. While Alibaba was the first to develop these finance innovations, it was certainly not the only one, and as we will also discuss in Chapter 7 and 8, competitors like Baidu, Tencent, Xiaomi and LeEco all became active competitors. Since China's regulatory environment is indeed dynamic and continuously changing, recent reforms and new regulations may hinder Internet finance in China. Moreover, Ant Financial also faces operational issues of limited sources of funds, product innovation, risk control and trust and Internet security. Nevertheless, there are still plenty of untapped opportunities for innovation.

References

Alipay, 2013. Zhi fu bao shou ji yong hu chao 1 yi, qian bao yong hu jie jin 1 yi [Alipay mobile payment users over 100 million and Alipay wallet users also about 100 million]. Available at: https://ab.alipay.com/i/dashiji.htm. Accessed 20/12/2016 [in Chinese].

Alizila, 2013. Alipay Yu'ebao is largest money market fund in China. Available at: http://www.alizila.com/alipay-yue-bao-is-largest-money-market-fund-in-china/. Accessed 20/12/2016.

Alizila, 2014. Alibaba.com and seven big Chinese banks offering loans to small exporters. Available at: http://www2.alizila.com/alibabacom-and-7-big-chinese-banks-offering-loans-small-exporters-0#sthash.168owRkq.dpuf. Accessed 20/12/2016.

Analysys, 2016. 2016 Shang ban nian zhong guo di san fang zhi fu shi chang [China's third party payment market in the first half of 2016]. Available at: https://www.puhuijia.com/industryInfo/116665.html. Accessed 20/12/2016 [in Chinese].

Caijing, 2014. Zhong guo ying zi yin hang jian guan yan jiu: A li ba ba jin rong [Research on China's shadow banks: Alibaba finance]. Available at: http://column.caijing.com.cn/2014-05-04/114151561.html. Accessed 20/12/2016 [in Chinese].

China Finance and Economy Times, 2017. Zhong an bao xian chan pin shou re peng [Products of Zhongan Insurance are popular]. Available at: http://economy.china.com/jykx/news/11179727/20170210/24006576.html. Accessed 20/12/2016 [in Chinese].

China Statistical Yearbook, 2016. *National Bureau of Statistics of China.* Available at: http://www.stats.gov.cn/tjsj/ndsj/2016/indexeh.htm. Accessed 11/02/2017.

CNNIC, 2012. 2012 Nian shang ban nian di san fang zhi fu shi chang yong hu fu gai qing kuang bi jiao [User coverage comparision of the third party market in the first half of 2012]. *China Internet Network Information Center.* Available at: http://www.cnnic.cn/hlwfzyj/fxszl/fxswz/201209/t20120924_36467.htm. Accessed 20/12/2016 [in Chinese].

Csai News, 2015. Hu lian wang jin rong zheng xin ti xi jian she de xian zhuang he fa zhan jian yi [Internet finance credit system situation report and directive]. Available at: http://www.csai.cn/p2pzixun/975173.html. Accessed 20/12/2016 [in Chinese].

Financial Times, 2017a. How finance is being taken over by tech. Available at: https://www.ft.com/content/2f6f5ba4-dc97-11e6-86ac-f253db7791c6. Accessed 19/02/2017.

Financial Times, 2017b. China mobile payments dwarf US volumes. Available at: https://www.ft.com/content/00585722-ef42-11e6-930f-061b01e23655. Accessed 20/02/2017.

Financial Times, 2016. China's Zhongan sees scope for offbeat insurance. Available at: https://www.ft.com/content/bee51a52-accd-11e6-9cb3-bb8207902122. Accessed 24/02/2017.

Financial Times, 2015. Alibaba finance arm launches online bank. Available at: http://www.ft.com/cms/s/0/e76198d2-1b26-11e5-8201-cbdb03d71480.html#ixzz3w6ByEYNs. Accessed 20/12/2016.

Financial Times, 2013. Alibaba: shaking up Chinese finance. Available at: http://blogs.ft.com/beyond-brics/2013/07/01/alibaba-shaking-up-chinese-finance/. Accessed 20/12/2016.

Greeven, M.J., Yue, T., Wei, W., Koene, B. and Hou, S., 2016, 'Alibaba's growth frenzy: Pioneer in China's Internet financial service', The Case Centre, Reference no. 116-0065-1. Available at: http://www.thecasecentre.org/educators/products/view?id=136214.

Hexun, 2011. Zhi fu bao kuai jie zhi fu yong hu nian di you wang po 4000 wan [Alipay users may reach over 40 million by the end of this year]. Available at: http://www.ebrun.com/20111027/34796.shtml. Accessed 20/12/2016 [in Chinese].

Jinghua Times, 2006. Zhong guo you zheng yu a li ba ba zhan lue he zuo [The strategic partnership between China Post and Alibaba]. Available at: http://news.163.com/06/1123/01/30J0H0EM000120GU.html. Accessed 20/12/2016 [in Chinese].

Netease, 2014. Zhi fu bao qian bao yong hu shu da 1.9 yi [Alipay has 190 million users]. Available at: http://news.163.com/14/1019/05/A8T6JRAJ00014Q4P.html. Accessed 20/12/2016 [in Chinese].

Peking University Business Review, 2007. A li ba ba: zhong guo te se de B2B mo shi [Alibaba: Chinese characteristic B2B mode]. Available at: http://finance.sina.com.cn/leadership/case/20070612/17553685119.shtml. Accessed 20/12/2016 [in Chinese].

Qianzhan, 2013. Zhong xiao qi ye rong zi xu qiu nan duo di shi shui 'jin rong cang chu' [Financing needs of SMEs are difficult, testing the water with 'financial storage']. Available at: http://www.qianzhan.com/analyst/detail/220/131209-cd58cfd7.html. Accessed 20/12/2016 [in Chinese].

Sina, 2015. Zhi fu bao qian bao yue huo yue yong hu shu 2.7 yi [Alipay monthly active users reached 270 million]. Available at: http://tech.sina.com.cn/i/2015-04-22/doc-iawzuney4040969.shtml. Accessed 20/12/2016 [in Chinese].

Sohu, 2016. 2015 hu lian wang bao xian cheng ji dan [Internet insurance report card 2015]. Available at: http://mt.sohu.com/20160205/n436959694.shtml. Accessed 20/12/2016 [in Chinese].

Startup-Partner, 2015. Hu lian wang jin rong "zhong an baoxian - zhong an zai xian" huo mo gen shi dan li A lun 9.34 yi mei yuan rong zi [Internet finance "Zhongan Insurance - Zhongan Online" raised A round 934 million USD from Morgan Stanley]. Available at: http://www.startup-partner.com/530.html. Accessed 20/12/2016 [in Chinese].

Tencent Finance, 2016. Cheng xin tong bai pi shu [Chengxintong white paper]. Available at: http://finance.qq.com/a/20160812/032319.htm. Accessed 20/12/2016 [in Chinese].

The World Fact Book, 2016. Washington, DC: Central Intelligence Agency. Available at: https://www.cia.gov/library/publications/the-world-factbook/index.html. Accessed 2/01/2017.

TechWeb, 2016. A li de zhao cai bao ye bei ju: ping tai huai zhang wei yue 3 ge yi. Available at: http://www.techweb.com.cn/internet/2016-12-26/2461376.shtml Accessed 10/02/2017 [in Chinese].

Worldbank, 2003. *Improving the investment climate in China*. Washington, The World Bank Group.

Zhang, Y., 2014. Zhi fu bao cheng shi ming ren zheng yong hu jin 3 yi [Alipay claimed to have about 300 million real-name registered users which makes it the largest mobile payment company globally]. *Xinhuanet*. Available at: http://news.xinhuanet.com/fortune/2014-02/08/c_119247927.htm. Accessed 20/01/2017 [in Chinese].

6

ALIBABA'S BUSINESS ECOSYSTEM GOING GLOBAL

6.1 Introduction

Ma Yun on more than one occasion stressed the international ambition of Alibaba; building a business ecosystem which can serve two billion consumers and millions of companies to sell global and buy global. To realize this ambition, Alibaba continues to invest in new and existing overseas operations including Alibaba.com international, a B2B ecommerce platform aiming to help Chinese SMEs to exhibit and market their products to the rest of the world; AliExpress, a cross border online marketplace positioned to sell Chinese goods to consumers all over the world; and Tmall Global, which helps foreign brands sell online directly to Chinese consumers. Alibaba is opening foreign branches and actively investing and acquiring companies in target markets as well as internationalizing its third party online payment Alipay and support services Alibaba Cloud. Although Alibaba Cloud is still generating limited revenues, it is one of the next potential drivers of growth abroad (Forbes, 2016).

Furthermore, recruiting top tier international talent has become a strategic priority. In August 2015, Alibaba Group appointed former Goldman Sachs vice chairman Michael Evans as president of Alibaba Group to lead the execution of the international strategy. Moreover, in order to foster the future international leaders of Alibaba, Alibaba initiated the Alibaba Global Leadership Academy (AGLA), a talent development program, aiming to cultivate Alibaba's global business leaders and cultural ambassadors, linking international markets with China. AGLA graduates are supposed to comprise the foundation for Alibaba's international business expansion.

The globalization of Alibaba's business ecosystem has already started. Based on our research, (see Section 1.4) and our BATXL database, we will discuss the motives of Alibaba's globalization in the context of the overall trend of China going global and then discuss four components of Alibaba's current globalization strategy and outcomes: 1) cross border ecommerce; 2) overseas subsidiaries; 3) service internationalization; and 4) overseas investments and acquisitions.

6.2 China going global: Motives of Alibaba

The ambition to globalize certainly exists in China, especially after decades of rapid domestic growth. In the *China's Innovation's Going Global Survey* by Veldhoen et al. (2014), over 80% of responding Chinese firms have the intention to expand abroad in the next ten years. This result fits the overall trend of strongly increasing outward foreign direct investment (OFDI) from China. China's OFDI has risen sharply since 2003 with an average annual growth rate of over 80% (MOFCOM, 2015) and has already risen to a record high of 170 billion USD in 2016, making it the world's third largest outward investor. The number of Chinese overseas acquisitions has more than doubled in the past five years and reached 742 deals and 107 billion USD in more than 70 countries in 2016 (China Investment Consulting Net, 2017).

China's globalization has been quick. Only in the 1990s, FDI officially became part of China's national economic development plan and the Chinese government started to actively encourage Chinese OFDI in order to explore overseas markets, increase the competitiveness of Chinese enterprises, and avoid foreign tariff barriers. Over 120 companies, termed 'global industry champions' by the Chinese government, accessed overseas investment programs between 1991 and 1997, including Sinopec, China Telecom, Lenovo and Haier. Then, after 2000 the Chinese government formally started the "Going abroad" policy aiming to develop internationally competitive enterprises, secure resources abroad, overcome intensified domestic competition and overcapacity in the domestic economy, acquire advanced technology to address competitive disadvantages such as brands and managerial know-how.

Driven by the many failed ventures abroad and limited returns to the domestic economy, the Chinese government now provides more guidance, focusing not only on cheap assets but increasingly on technology for domestic use, such as in the case of Geely's acquisition of Volvo, instead of only brand value. Moreover, the target industries and companies have also been changing over the years. In the early stage, state-owned enterprises played more important roles by investing mostly in natural resources and in the later stages, the target industries became more diverse while private companies participated in overseas investment more actively. Take China's OFDI to the US as an example; it increased three times to over 50 billion USD in 2016 compared to 2015. Moreover, the merger and acquisition activities by Chinese private companies played a key role. In particular, half of the OFDI has been invested in technology fields (People's Daily, 2017).

It is in this context that we assess the globalization of Alibaba's business ecosystem. The motives of Chinese companies going global are various (Child and Rodrigues, 2005), from resource seeking, to market and technology seeking. In the last decade the main actor in Chinese globalization has been the Chinese private firm, rather than the state owned firm, and also included a wide variety of SMEs. Therefore, the motivation, conditions and trends of globalization made Alibaba's global moves not surprising. According to our interviews and observations, Alibaba's motives for globalization are the following:

- Vision of Alibaba as a global business platform, competing globally rather than domestically
- Meeting new demands of existing domestic consumers for foreign products, especially from developed countries
- Opening new markets to satisfy the rising needs of foreign consumers for Chinese products, especially from developing countries
- Growth of the ecommerce ecosystem into new markets
- Preparing overseas stock listing to generate positive reputation effects while at the same time raising capital for further expansion
- Geographic diversification of the services such as Alipay and Alibaba Cloud to create scale effect and achieve worldwide expansion
- Upgrading technology of the ecommerce core and exploring technologies for complementary offerings in the ecosystem

In the following four sections we discuss Alibaba's four strategic activities in globalization: cross border ecommerce, setting up overseas branches, service internationalization and overseas investment and acquisition.

6.3 Cross border ecommerce: Pioneering a trend

It should not be forgotten that the origin of Alibaba is the leading global ecommerce platform Alibaba.com International, established in 1999. The focus has been on exporting Chinese goods. Alibaba is a real pioneer in cross border ecommerce in China, perhaps also globally. Nevertheless, with the 2007 launch of Taobao Global, a C2C import focused ecommerce platform, the domestic consumer ecommerce business outgrew its export focused B2B ecommerce and became the strategic business of Alibaba for over a decade. Only until 2013, Alibaba started to proactively pull the strings in cross border ecommerce again, with an eye on the overall cross border ecommerce trends in the country.

The growth of cross border ecommerce since 2010 cannot be ignored. The overall trade size of cross border ecommerce in China reached 5.4 trillion RMB in 2015 (CECRC, 2016). The export was dominant with a transaction volume of about 4.5 trillion RMB, while import was only less than 1 trillion RMB but with a much higher growth rate. Given the slowdown of China's export due to the weakening demand from countries and regions like Europe and Japan as well as other uncertainties of international trade, cross border ecommerce's role becomes more important for China's economy. In the past years, the Chinese government issued a series of policies promoting cross border ecommerce to upgrade traditional export. Meanwhile, import ecommerce is growing significantly since 2014 due to the boom of the more demanding middle class for foreign products. The capital markets also smell this opportunity and the pioneering import ecommerce ventures like Yangmatou, Xiaohongshu, and Mia.com all successfully raised large investments from venture capital funds.

Alibaba significantly expanded its cross border ecommerce activities since early 2013. In April 2013, AliExpress announced a plan to change its role by targeting not only small order business customers but also individual consumers outside of China, in particular focusing on Russia, India, Brazil and Eastern Europe initially. When it was launched in 2010, AliExpress was a small order focused B2B ecommerce platform, which not only displayed information like Alibaba.com, but also facilitated the whole trading process. However, until 2013, over 65% of buyers on AliExpress were individuals and it had a new strategic positioning, i.e. export focused retail ecommerce.

Then, in February 2014, Alibaba launched Tmall Global, a platform where overseas brands and merchants can sell their products directly to Chinese online consumers. Tmall Global started to build its brand network from Hong Kong, Taiwan and Japan to Europe, the USA, Australia and New Zealand. In April 2014 Tmall Global collaborated with the Ningbo bonded tax zone to guarantee a shorter delivery time for consumers. Within one year, big brands like Costco, Metro, Macy's, Sainsbury, Rakuten and Chemist Warehouse were all represented on Tmall Global. Riding the waves of the cross border ecommerce trend, Tmall Global saw a tenfold sales increase from the beginning to the end of 2014. By June 2015, Tmall Global had teamed up with 13 countries to build their curated shopping sites for selling popular products and specialties from selected companies to Chinese customers, including the USA, New Zealand, Australia, Switzerland and France. Moreover, in August 2015, after striking a strategic partnership with Chinese crowdsourcing translation platform 365 Fanyi, Alibaba went a step further to fully acquire the company, utilizing it to remove language barriers in cross border ecommerce business. By the end of 2016, it had attracted more than 14,500 foreign brands of over 3,700 product categories from over 60 countries and regions to open shops on it; in particular, 80% of these brands entered the Chinese market for the first time (Sohu, 2016).

Looking at the shopper profiles of Tmall Global in 2016, we see that most new shoppers are female consumers from tier 1 and tier 2 cities born in the 1980s, focusing on products like cosmetics, food, maternal and infant supplies. The interesting trend is that another new generation is quickly adopting overseas shopping: about half of the new consumers in 2016 are the youngsters born after 1990. This new generation has different living and shopping habits, more focused on personal quality of life and comfort (CBNdata, 2017).

Another trend that Tmall Global is playing into is the increasing international travel of Chinese consumers. In 2015 over 120 million Chinese had travelled overseas and accounted for 1.5 trillion RMB worth of overseas spending, while the market size of the overseas shopping for mainland customers reached 200 billion RMB. Tmall Global intends to transfer this to online overseas shopping via their platform, thereby increasing domestic consumption of overseas products. During the 11.11 shopping festival of 2016, initiated by Alibaba three years ago at a global scale, the total transaction volume reached 120 billion RMB in one day. On that day alone there were 47 million shoppers; within nine hours already surpassing last year's total transaction volume (Financial Times, 2016a). Alibaba has successfully groomed the import shoppers over the last several years and achieved consumption upgrading through cross border import focused ecommerce (China Consumer Net, 2016).

6.4 Setting up overseas branches: Greenfield attempts

Developing cross border ecommerce is not the only way for Alibaba to internationalize. Alibaba has also been attempting to set up overseas branches (greenfield approach) in recent years. In February 2014, Vendio and Auctiva, two ecommerce service providers for online sellers, which were acquired by Alibaba in 2010, were set to launch a new ecommerce site named 11Main in the US market. 11 Main is positioned as a boutique ecommerce business, offering high quality products from selected merchants in the fashion, electronic and jewellery industries. It aimed to build a compelling platform which can offer different user experiences as compared to dominant ecommerce companies like eBay and Amazon. However, the first time direct expansion of Alibaba's core business did not seem very successful. By June 2015, 11Main merged with American ecommerce site Open Sky. Alibaba declared to have 37% of the newly merged company and will let it run independently. The reasons for the drawback of the trial could be multiple: distance between the local team and headquarters, highly competitive and saturated market, different business approach compared to China and lack of logistics advantages unlike China. Moreover, according to the vice chairman of Alibaba Joseph Cai, the key question is whether or not they should have a specific platform for the American market. On the long run, probably they would need to and they also have a strong interest in the American market. However, at the moment they prioritize cross border ecommerce, from the relatively familiar Chinese business context (Sohu, 2015).

Nevertheless, Alibaba did not stop its efforts to expand overseas branches. In December 2015, Alibaba built the SMILE platform in India to provide lending, logistics and technical services for Indian SMEs, hoping the small but fast expanding ecommerce sector in India would have the same explosive growth as in China. In May 2016, Alibaba opened its Benelux HQ in Amsterdam and hired the former general manager of one of Holland's largest retail chains. Early in February 2017, Alibaba announced the establishment of an Australian headquarters to facilitate Australian and New Zealand businesses. Altogether, libaba is expanding its footsteps abroad. In combination with the newly nched global talent strategy, Alibaba's overall overseas presence and reputa- is improving.

6.5 Service internationalization: Reaching global scale

Besides expanding cross border ecommerce and setting up overseas branches, Alibaba is also internationalizing its services Alibaba Cloud and Alipay in the past year. Initially Alibaba Cloud opened a data centre in Hong Kong in 2014 and doubled its capacity in 2017 (Forbes, 2017). In March 2015, Alibaba Cloud opened its first overseas data centre in Silicon Valley. Two months later, Alibaba Cloud established a joint venture YVOLV in Dubai with a local company Meraas, aiming to sell system integration services to companies and government organizations in the Middle East and North Africa. In June 2015, Alibaba Cloud declared its Marketplace Alliance Program, aiming to find global partners to build cloud ecosystem and offer one stop cloud solution. The first batch of its global partners included Intel, SingTel, Equinix and PCCW (Alizila, 2015). In September 2015, Alibaba Cloud opened its Singapore data centre (Alizila, 2015). In 2016, another four new data centres in Europe, Australia, Japan and Middle East were established. In the same year, it founded a joint venture, SB Cloud Corporation with SoftBank, the Tokyo based Internet incumbent, to expand cloud services in Japan (Alibaba, 2016). As of September 30, 2016, the number of Alibaba Cloud subscribers increased by 108% to 650,000 and revenue increased by 130% to reach 1.5 billion RMB. In 2016 Alibaba Cloud competed in a global big data competition 'Sort Benchmark' and won in the category CloudSort, breaking the record of former winner AWS, the Amazon Web Service. After 7 years of development, Alibaba Cloud has become the largest public cloud service provider in China with 2.3 million clients. Internationally it is strongly competing with AWS and Microsoft Cloud Service Azure.

Besides Alibaba Cloud, Alipay, as one of the key success factors of Alibaba's ecommerce business, the core of Alibaba's finance arm Ant Financial as well as the crucial glue of Alibaba's ecosystem, is expanding internationally. Its expansion plays a significant role in the ecosystem going global. In October 2013, Alipay started to support an overseas shopping tax refund in South Korea and expanded this service to Singapore and Europe in 2014. Now, it's available in over 150 countries and regions. In April 2014, Alipay announced it will be added as a payment option on Yahoo! Shopping Japan and also reached cooperation with Japanese ecommerce giant Rakuten to add Alipay as a payment option for purchases on Rakuten Global Market. In November 2014, Alipay's 'foreign direct purchase' ePass service went live in the US, which means Chinese consumers can shop directly online from the biggest American department stores such as Neiman Marcus, Macy's, Bloomingdales and Sack's Fifth Avenue (TechNode, 2014). Alipay has joined forces with One97 Communications, which oversees Paytm, India's largest mobile wallet provider, to fund payment services in the Indian ecommerce market. In December 2016 Alibaba announced it had signed deals that allow Chinese consumers to use Alipay in over 900,000 merchants in Europe (Financial Times, 2016b). Recent expansions of the service abroad including Alipay became available as payment options in Finair's flights since 2017.

Although Alipay's internationalization is successful to the extent that the Chinese consumers have expanded their use of Alipay abroad, it has not yet having succeeded in attracting overseas users. Nevertheless, Alipay declared its internationalization ambition at the Money 2020 conference in Copenhagen in April 2016 that within ten years, Alipay will serve 2 billion users globally with more than half from outside of China, which also clearly indicates that the internationalization of Alipay will still be a strategic focus in the coming years (China Net Tech, 2016).

6.6 Overseas investment and acquisitions: Diversification

Overseas investment is also a crucial part of Alibaba's internationalization strategy, as Alibaba's overseas investment data from our BATXL database suggests. By the end of 2016, 44 deals, which is about 23% of its total investments, were outside of China. As shown in Figure 6.1, Alibaba's steps of going abroad by investments were slow before 2013. It acquired American ecommerce service providers Vendio and Auctiva in 2010, and bought Oncard, an Australia third party payment company, in 2011. Two years later Alibaba had another three investments in the US, i.e. application search company Quixey (50 million USD), vertical ecommerce company Fanatics (a total financing of 150 million USD together with other investors) and ecommerce logistics provider ShopRunner (70 million USD). It's notable that the first three overseas deals are all acquisitions, two in the US, one in Australia, focusing on strengthening its core business ecommerce and third party payment. The later three investments were all in the US and mostly in ecommerce related fields. It indicates the early phase of Alibaba's overseas strategy intended to expand its own core business to the US market by means of acquisitions and strategic investments. Another interesting fact is that the three companies Vendio, Auctiva and ShopRunner were all former ecommerce service providers for eBay and its

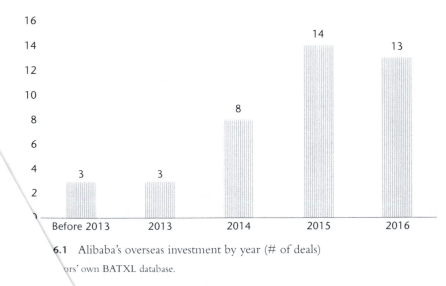

6.1 Alibaba's overseas investment by year (# of deals)

ors' own BATXL database.

sellers, implying Alibaba paid close attention to its American peers and tried to find opportunities from eBay's business network as well.

In 2014, Alibaba sped up its overseas investment to eight deals in total. Most of the investments are still in the US, such as a 15 million USD investment to 1stdibs, an American specialized ecommerce vendor of luxurious products; a 215 million investment USD to Tango, an popular mobile video communication application; a 120 million USD invested to Kabam, a mobile game developer who developed 'The Kind of the Ring' series of games and planned to enter the Chinese market; and an investment to Lyft, the competitor of Uber, a taxi hailing application. These investments were believed to have strengthened Alibaba's presence in the US and to have expanded its reach outside of China as a deliberate preparation before Alibaba went public on the NYSE in September 2014.

However, Alibaba's eyes were not exclusively on the US, as the Group also acquired a 10% stake in Singapore Post Limited for 249 million USD and a security software development company V-Key in Singapore in 2014. It seems slowly Alibaba is turning its attention from the USA to Southeast Asia, with a bigger variety of target fields. The diverse trend in terms of location as well as field becomes more obvious in 2015 and 2016. Although Alibaba still did large investments in the US, such as Snapchat, a popular photo sharing application, and Zulily and Jet.com, both are again ecommerce companies, it expanded target countries to Japan, India, Hong Kong and South Korea with investments in location based services, culture and entertainment and software tool, among others.

In particular, Hong Kong became an important targets country. Alibaba acquired South China Morning Post, one of the most well known English Media originated in Greater China, and invested in ecommerce companies Grana, Yeechoo, Shopline, mobile logistics platform GoGoVan as well as AGTech, a sports lottery operator. India is also a strategic focus for Alibaba's overseas investments. The investments in India are in fields like ecommerce (Snapdeal, one of the largest ecommerce platforms in India), finance (Paytm, the largest online payment supplier and one of the most valuable start-ups in India), as well as hardware (smartphone producer Micromax).

Another notable target country is Israel. Alibaba invested four Israeli companies, including QR code generating software tool developer Visualead, ecommerce search venture Twiggle, Internet security service provider Thetaray and augmented reality company Infinity. It seems that Alibaba is exploring possible frontier technologies in Israel, where companies are well known for innovation in China.

Besides investments, Alibaba also tried to connect to the local entrepreneurial environment in other ways. For instance, in November 2015, Alibaba launched the Hong Kong Entrepreneurs Fund of about 129 million USD and Taiwan Entrepreneurs Fund, valued about 309 million USD, on the same day. Moreover, in December 2016, Ma Yun together with Bill Gates and other international technology industry leaders established a 1 billion USD Breakthrough Energy Ventures Fund to invest in companies developing cutting edge energy technologies (Bishop, 2016).

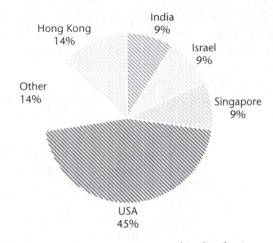

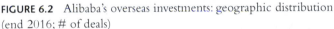

FIGURE 6.2 Alibaba's overseas investments: geographic distribution (end 2016; # of deals)

Source: authors' own BATXL database.

By the end of 2016, about 45% of Alibaba's overseas investments were in the USA, 40% were in Southeast Asia, including Hong Kong, India, Singapore, South Korea, Thailand) and the rest scattered around the world; see Figure 6.2. This suggests that Alibaba's overseas expansion targeted the US market rather than the European market as part of their developed market expansion; suggesting that the US is leading in ecommerce developments, as compared to Europe. Emerging market expansion is mostly nearby Southeast Asia. Interesting to note that Alibaba is not active in large emerging markets such as Brazil and Russia in terms of investments but is active in the cross border ecommerce expansion as we can see in Section 6.2.

In terms of sector distribution, Alibaba's overseas investments include at least 13 different sectors, ecommerce being the largest one. Furthermore, our database shows that the sector distribution of international investments is similar to the domestic investments. Besides ecommerce, culture and entertainment, finance, hardware, LBS and logistics are the largest receivers. Moreover, it must be noted that our database shows that the investments abroad are rather diverse and tend to be large scale, more mature phase investments with less than 20% in early phase start-ups.

6.7 Insights: Alibaba's globalization motives, strategy and outcomes

The largest component of Alibaba's global strategy is comprehensive cross border ecommerce. Alibaba's cross border ecommerce business includes AliExpress (foreign SMEs and consumers buying Chinese products, B2B and B2C), Tmall Global (Chinese consumers buying foreign products, B2C), Taobao Global (Chinese consumers buying foreign products, C2C) and Alibaba.com international (foreign business source Chinese factories/suppliers, B2B). Moreover, in particular the year 2014 has been important for the globalization of ecommerce. Part of the reason is the preparation for its IPO in the USA and associated heavy investments in a relatively short time frame. However, as expected by the dynamics of Alibaba business ecosystem, in 2015 Alibaba started to expand deeper into Southeast Asian markets, especially in light of the internationalization of the smart logistics network Cainiao, of which Alibaba is a key founding partner; see details in Section 4.3.

Alibaba's globalization motives are manifold. In particular, it is important to realize that the globalization of Alibaba's business ecosystem cannot be compared to globalizing one company, as is traditionally the focus of strategic management. The complex and many motives of Alibaba's globalization, as illustrated in Table 6.1, include market, technology, capital, reputation and scale. As predicted, such motives require a more complex and comprehensive globalization strategy.

When assessing the globalization strategy we conclude that Alibaba has a diverse approach, as illustrated in Table 6.2. While each of the four global activities have specific regional and sectoral focus areas, combined they form a comprehensive approach to globalize Alibaba's business ecosystem. The cross border ecommerce first focused on Russia, India, Brazil and Eastern Europe with AliExpress and later, with Tmall Global, moved into Hong Kong, Taiwan, Japan to Western Europe, the USA, Australia and New Zealand, thereby creating a comprehensive cross border ecommerce ecosystem that is a true extension of Alibaba's domestic ecommerce ecosystem. Both Alibaba Cloud and Alipay's internationalization is truly global while Alibaba's overseas subsidiaries are currently limited and focused on developed

TABLE 6.1 Motives for Alibaba's business ecosystem globalization

Motive categories	*Motives*
Vision	• Vision of Alibaba as a global business platform, competing globally rather than domestically
Market expansion	• Meeting new demands of existing domestic consumers for foreign products, especially from developed countries • Opening new markets to satisfy the rising needs of foreign consumers for Chinese products, especially from developing countries • Growth of the ecommerce ecosystem into a new large market, focus on the developed USA but also attention to emerging India
Access to capital	• Preparing overseas stock listing to generate positive reputation effects while at the same time raising capital for further expansion
Scale	• Geographic diversification of services like Alibaba Cloud and Alipay to create scale effects, worldwide expansion
Technology	• Upgrading technology of the ecommerce core and exploring technologies for complementary offerings in the ecosystem

TABLE 6.2 Global strategy of Alibaba: four components

Cross border ecommerce: Comprehensive and leading	Overseas subsidiaries: Solid step into foreign markets
<ul><li>'import / export'</li><li>Tmall Global: selling foreign products to Chinese consumers</li><li>AliExpress: selling Chinese products to foreign consumers</li><li>Alibaba.com: sourcing Chinese products to foreign business customers</li></ul>	<ul><li>'greenfield'</li><li>Failed greenfield attempt in the USA</li><li>Alibaba Cloud technology development centers in the USA, Dubai, Japan</li><li>Support for overseas SMEs in India</li><li>Market support and expansion in Benelux region and Australia</li></ul>
Service internationalization: Creating scale and synergy	**Overseas investments and acquisitions: A diversified approach**
<ul><li>'hybrid partnerships'</li><li>Acquisition of overseas payment services</li><li>Overseas shopping Alipay tax refund service</li><li>Partnerships with local companies in the US, Japan, Europe and Middle East</li><li>Establishment of Alibaba Cloud data centres in Hong Kong, the US, Japan, Germany, Dubai, and Australia</li></ul>	<ul><li>'acquisition'</li><li>16% early phase investments, the majority is mature phase</li><li>Overseas investment targets the US market (45%) rather than the European market</li><li>Focus on nearby East Asian markets for new growth and market access</li><li>Focus to expand current ecommerce ecosystem</li></ul>

markets like the USA, Japan and Benelux while only recently entering the Indian, Middle East and African markets. Lastly, it is interesting to notice that investment and acquisition is focused on the USA and nearby Asian markets (with the exception of Israel) and completely not in other emerging markets such as Brazil and Russia or European markets for that matter.

When assessing the outcomes of Alibaba's globalization strategy, we can conclude that given the short time frame, Alibaba has booked many significant successes, as illustrated in Table 6.3. Our findings in this chapter suggest that Alibaba's business ecosystem has made significant strides in internationalization. While it is not an easy task to build up a business ecosystem abroad that is as deeply embedded in China's domestic market, at least we see that Alibaba's diverse strategic approaches (combining partnerships, greenfield subsidiaries, investments and cross border ecommerce) are a significant attempt to build up a global business ecosystem. The starting point is to cleverly utilize Alibaba's domestic consumers that increasingly travel and live abroad to internationalize services such as Alipay and foreign import ecommerce. As analyzed in Section 6.3, Alibaba has successfully upgraded domestic consumers to shopping across borders via online platforms and committed the majority of large international brands and companies to be visible on their platform. Moreover, following Chinese clients abroad and setting up services such as Alibaba Cloud seem to be an important step for Alibaba's globalization. Lastly, the focus on the

TABLE 6.3 Outcomes of Alibaba's global strategy (end 2016)

Cross border ecommerce	Overseas subsidiaries
• Tmall: 14,500 foreign brands of over 3,700 product categories from over 60 countries. Its transactions increased 179% in 2015, the largest overseas shopping platform in China • AliExpress: 34 million sellers and 100 million buyers, 243 countries covered	Six subsidiaries covering the USA, Europe, Middle East/Africa, Japan, India, Australia
Service internationalization	**Overseas investments and acquisitions**
• 150 countries tax refund service • Alipay online payment and LBS platforms for 10 international airports • Covering six strategic regions by establishing the international Alibaba Cloud data centres • Gained reputation by winning the international cloud technology competition	• About 7 billion USD invested • 44 overseas deals in ten countries • Investment commitments in 13 sectors while predominantly ecommerce

Source: Alibaba Group, 2016

US market for ecommerce technology and platform investment indicates both the commitment of Alibaba to enter the US market but also the understanding that it needs to build up a strong local ecosystem of ecommerce companies. The next step will be to convince foreign customers to adopt Alibaba's services.

References

Alibaba Group, 2016. *Alibaba Group Financial Reports 2016*, Hong Kong, Alibaba Group. Available at: http://www.alibabagroup.com/en/ir/secfilings. Accessed 22/02/2017.

Alizila, 2015. A li yun qi dong quan qiu he zuo huo ban ji hua [Alibaba Cloud initiated the global partnership program]. Available at: http://www.alibabagroup.com/cn/news/article?news=p150608. Accessed 20/12/2016 [in Chinese].

Bishop, T. 2016. Bill Gates, Jack Ma and others form $1B venture fund to invest in cutting-edge energy technologies. *Geekwire.com*. Available at: http://www.geekwire.com/2016/bill-gates-jack-ma-others-form-1b-venture-fund-invest-cutting-edge-energy-technologies/. Accessed 20/12/2016.

CBNdata, 2017. 2016 Jin kou xiao fei bao gao [2016 import consumption report]. Available at: http://www.yicai.com/news/5204653.html. Accessed 20/02/2017 [in Chinese].

CECRC, 2016. 2015 Nian du zhong guo dian zi shang wu shi chang shu ju [2015 China ecommerce market data]. *China Electronic Commerce Research Center*. Available at: http://b2b.toocle.com/zt/2015ndbg/. Accessed 20/12/2016 [in Chinese].

China Consumer Net, 2016. Tian mao guo ji shai 2016 cheng ji dan [Tmall Global shows its 2016 report card]. Available at: http://www.zhiliangcn.com/news/201612/88191.html. Accessed 20/12/2016 [in Chinese].

China Investment Consulting Net, 2017. Shang wu bu: 2016 nian wo guo dui wai tou zi he zuo cheng xian wu da te dian [Ministry of Commerce: in 2016 China's OFDI has five features]. Available at: http://www.ocn.com.cn/chanjing/201701/hplay17142351.shtml. Accessed 20/02/2017 [in Chinese].

China Net Tech, 2016. Zhi fu bao guo ji hua mu biao [Alipay's internationalization goal]. Available at: http://news.k618.cn/tech/201604/t20160412_7124816.html. Accessed 20/12/2016 [in Chinese].

Child, J. and Rodrigues, S.B., 2005. 'The internationalization of Chinese firms: A case for theoretical extension?', *Management and Organization Review*, 1 (3), pp. 381–410.

Forbes, 2017. With cloud, Alibaba follows the 'build it and they will come' approach. Available at: https://www.forbes.com/sites/jaysomaney/2017/02/13/with-cloud-alibaba-follows-the-build-it-and-they-will-come-approach/#611d1d47191b. Accessed 20/02/2017.

Forbes, 2016. Can Alibaba's cloud business be its next driver of growth? Available at: https://www.forbes.com/sites/greatspeculations/2016/05/09/can-alibabas-cloud-business-be-its-next-driver-of-growth/#5ade8ed176ed. Accessed 20/02/2017.

Financial Times, 2016a. Alibaba's Singles Day sale worth record $17.8bn. Available at: https://www.ft.com/content/8aa13ac6-a7b1-11e6-8b69-02899e8bd9d1. Accessed 30/11/2016

Financial Times, 2016b. Alipay signs deals for expansion in Europe. Available at: https://www.ft.com/content/f6459164-bbca-11e6-8b45-b8b81dd5d080. Accessed 20/02/2017.

MOFCOM, 2015. Statistics of FDI in China in January-December 2014. *Ministry of Commerce People's Republic of China*. Available at: http://english.mofcom.gov.cn/article/statistic/foreigninvestment/201504/20150400942402.shtml. Accessed 20/12/2016.

People's Daily, 2017. Zhong guo 2016 nian dui wai tou zi chuang li shi ji lu [China's OFDI hit a history record in 2016]. Available at: http://finance.people.com.cn/n1/2017/0113/c1004-29022519.html. Accessed 20/02/2017 [in Chinese].

Sohu, 2016. Tian mao guo ji he xin shu ju da bao guang [Explosure of Tmall Global's core data]. Availbale at: http://mt.sohu.com/20160203/n436822049.shtml. Accessed 20/12/2016 [in Chinese].

Sohu, 2015. Zai mei dian shang zhi lu bu shun, a li ba ba chu shou 11Main [A drawback of its ecommerce in the US, Alibaba sold 11Main]. Available at: http://it.sohu.com/20150623/n415486133.shtml. Accessed 20/12/2016 [in Chinese].

TechNode, 2014. U.S. department stores open doors to Alipay. Available at: http://technode.com/2014/11/21/us-department-stores-open-doors-alipay/. Accessed 20/12/2016.

Veldhoen, S., Mansson, A., Peng, B., Yip, G.S. and Han, J., 2014. *China's innovation's going global: 2014 China innovation survey*, strategy and CEIBS Center on China Innovation, Shanghai.

PART III

Beyond Alibaba: the leading Chinese ecosystems of Baidu, Tencent, Xiaomi, and LeEco

7

THE BUSINESS ECOSYSTEMS OF BAIDU AND TENCENT

7.1 Introduction

China's business landscape has at least four business ecosystems competing with Alibaba's business ecosystem: Baidu, Tencent, Xiaomi and LeEco. Many of these are growing as fast as Alibaba; expanding internationally and disrupting markets across industries. In this chapter we describe the transformation of the business ecosystems of Baidu and Tencent. Baidu and Tencent were established around the same time as Alibaba. While Alibaba started as an ecommerce platform, Baidu started as a search engine and Tencent focused on instant messaging. Together these three companies are known in China as BAT. Although they originally had their own business focus, they have met more than one time in the market; especially in the last years BAT started their extensive business diversification. Based on the extant Chinese publications on Baidu and Tencent and our research as indicated in Sections 1.3–1.4, in this chapter we discuss first Baidu and how founder Li Yanhong has built a business ecosystem around search and data. Then, we will discuss the case of Tencent and how its founder Ma Huateng has developed a digital communication and entertainment empire. For both cases we will not only describe the early development of the business ecosystem but pay specific attention to their business diversification and internationalization. The next chapter will then discuss the business ecosystems of Xiaomi and LeEco, the newcomers in the world of BAT. Chapter 9 provides a detailed comparative analysis of the five business ecosystems.

7.2 The ecosystem of Baidu

Baidu is China's largest online search engine with a focus on Chinese language search. In China's online search market, Baidu has 660 million active monthly users (September 2016) and 260 million overseas (December 2015), according to Baidu's financial reports. This represents 93% online search penetration with China's total number of netizens around 720 million. The total revenues of Baidu in 2015 reached 10 billion USD with a 35% year-on-year growth. Baidu's market capitalization is 58 billion USD (February 2017). However, Baidu is no longer just an online search engine. By 2016 the company boasted successful businesses in Internet finance, digital healthcare, online education, location based services, driverless cars and many others. *MIT Technology Review* recognized Baidu as one of the top 50 most intelligent companies worldwide in 2016.

7.2.1 Origin of Baidu: Li Yanhong

Li Yanhong was born (1968) in Yangquan City, Shanxi Province, with four sisters. He studied at Peking University and graduated in information management in 1991. Then he went abroad to study at New York University of Buffalo and majored in computer science. Equipped with academic talent he had considered pursuing a PhD but in the end chose to go for a corporate career. He started working as a consultant in a subsidiary of Dow Jones in New York, focusing on financial data analysis.

In 1997, Li Yanhong left Wall Street and moved to his dream town Silicon Valley to join a start-up, a pioneering Internet search engine Infoseek, on the invitation of the Taiwanese CTO William Jiang. In popular media Li Yanhong was often honored as creating the second generation Infoseek technology. However, more interesting is that he participated in the World Internet Conference in 1998 and met the two young founders of Google. In a follow-up meeting with many search engine focused technologists, the Google founders allegedly consulted Mr. Li, who was considered a technology expert, with many technology related questions. He never realized that a few years later, Google would outcompete Infoseek and Yahoo! and become the competitor of his later established company Baidu. Later in the same year Disney became a 40% shareholder of Infoseek, changing the company culture and also indirectly motivating Li to move on. In 1999, he decided to return to China and start his own venture.

Together with his friend and alumni Xu Yong, Li Yanhong started to search angel investors, initially in the USA. Endorsed by William Jiang who thought Li Yanhong to be top three search engine technologist in the world, they got 1.25 million USD angel investment and founded Baidu in Beijing in 2000. Within the same year, he successfully got the technology outsourcing contracts from Sina, Sohu, NetEase and Tom as well as his A round investment 10 million USD. In 2001, Baidu announced the first service: Baidu Search. At that time, Google had already entered the Chinese market a year earlier with a Chinese Google search engine.

7.2.2 The core of the ecosystem: Search technology

Baidu strongly competed with Google, especially in 2001–2002. In 2001 Baidu also started to promote the revenue model based on paid listings, i.e. a bidding system for advertisers on how much they would be willing to pay to appear at the top of results in response to specific searches. Then, Baidu announced a 'flash plan' to compete with Google in China in early 2002. The purpose of the flash plan was to compete with Google on search technology within nine months after launching the plan. Baidu was still a start-up at this stage and Google already a strong player with five million users in China. Located next to Peking University and employing many local graduates and students, Baidu was speeding up their development with 15 core engineers versus the many engineers of Google in China. In June 2003 the China Computer Education Newspaper organized a public competition between Baidu and Google and 55% of the over 10,000 users chose Baidu as the stronger Chinese search engine. In many ways, their flash plan had worked and the small local start-up outcompeted Google on technology. Baidu became the top Chinese search portal and top four Chinese Internet company; the others being Sina, Sohu and NetEase (Niubb, 2015). It is important to realize that this was well before the Chinese government started to control the Internet in China and block Google services; Baidu did by no means 'win' in China due to the protective measures of the Chinese government, as is often thought. In fact, Baidu, outcompeted Google on their own turf: search technology. Baidu Search was there to stay but it would take another decade for Baidu to make the next technological leap, i.e. artificial intelligence (AI).

In May 2014 Baidu attracted Andrew Ng, the former founder of Google AI, associate professor at Stanford University, as the key scientist to lead the Baidu Research Academy: AI Lab (Silicon Valley), Deep Learning Lab (Beijing) and Big Data Lab (Beijing). In fact, one month before Andrew Ng's joining, Li Yanhong already claimed that the Baidu Brain, an early product of Baidu's AI research project, had the intelligence of a 2-to 3-year-old child, indicating Baidu has already made quite some progress in this field. By the end of 2015, the Baidu Driverless Car, another application of its AI technology, finished the road test. Moreover, Baidu successfully developed a Deep Speech Two voice recognition system, which has been ranked as top ten breakthrough technologies in 2016 by *MIT Technology Review*. Moreover, China, but Baidu in particular, is widely considered to have gained on the US in AI technology (*The New York Times*, 2017). Clearly the focus of Baidu is again and still on developing pioneering technology; competing with Google and Microsoft rather than Alibaba and Tencent. Nevertheless, AI is not yet profitable and it is a bet on the future of this technology.

7.2.3 Extending the ecosystem: Complementary services for B2B and B2C

The core of Baidu's ecosystem is Baidu Search. However, in the first decade Baidu developed a large range of services for consumers and businesses that are complementary to Baidu Search. One type of complementary business is community based service. Early community services for consumers include the successful Baidu Tieba, launched in 2003, and Baidu Knows, an online search based interactive Q&A platform. Tieba is an online community covering all kinds of interesting topics.

It is noteworthy that Baidu paid a lot of attention to user generated content (UGC), especially considering the limited amount of content available on the Chinese Internet at that time. Google, on the contrary, focused mostly on developing search technology. Perhaps this is another part of the explanation of Baidu's success versus Google. The larger market share gap of Baidu (~60%) and Google (~25%) showed the result of the ongoing competition between the two companies; note that this is still before the Chinese government interfered with competition in the Internet market. In 2008 Baidu announced the community strategy to further expand and consolidate the success of the community services. By 2017, Baidu offered over 60 vertical search community service products. Next to community services for consumers, Baidu had launched many other search related services such as Baidu Maps (2008), Baidupedia (2008), Baidu Music (2012), Baidu Archive (2009) and Baidu Scholar (2014), among others, most of which are successful.

Besides consumer focused services, Baidu also offers business services for websites or developers, including Baidu Cloud Observation, which monitors website safety; Baidu Index, which performs key words data analysis; Baidu API Store, which provides API service for developers, among others. One relatively large offering is the Baidu Alliance which started early on, right after they initiated the paid listing revenue model in 2002. It is a search promotion collaboration which facilitates any online site or portal to become a marketing spot for promotion and the participating sites receive a commission per click via their site. In total Baidu has developed over 25 business oriented services for websites and developers and this constitutes a substantial part of Baidu's business ecosystem.

7.2.4 Growth by related diversification: Innovation, incubation, investment

Baidu's diversification into related but diverse fields of business started to take off in 2011. Although Baidu Games started already in 2007 and Baidu ecommerce You'a started in 2008, both had little impact and failed. Baidu's growth is driven by, on the one hand, the peer pressure by Alibaba and Tencent; on the other hand, a strategic need to diversify beyond the core of search business and find new revenue streams. Baidu employed three mechanisms to diversify into different sectors successfully. First of all, Baidu had initiated several innovative products and services. These are developed mostly by Baidu itself and focus on new product development. Second, Baidu has invested significantly in new companies and technologies. Third, Baidu initiated an incubation strategy called 'Baidu Entrepreneurship Centre' for Internet entrepreneurs in 2013. So far, five cities in China have the Baidu Entrepreneurship Centres with over 100 venture teams participating in incubation programs.

According to observers, Baidu has signficantly diversified into the following four business areas: digital healthcare, online education, Internet finance and location based services. These are the new nodes in the Baidu ecosystem, the new cores around which subsystems develop. These new cores are developed by innovation, incubation and investment.

Baidu has been actively promoting digital healthcare since 2013. The first initiative was an online consultation platform, later named Baidu Health. In the same year they started running Du Life, a smart wearables platform, integrating various wearable products by Baidu's cloud service and the same brand. In the following years Baidu developed a variety of services such as Baidu Healthcare Brain (AI diagnosis online consultancy), Baidu Medical Science (repository of medical knowledge for doctors), Baidu Yitu (medical picture scan community for doctors), and Yaozhida (pharmaceutical ecommerce). Moreover, Baidu has also been rather active in developing collaborations with other stakeholders in the healthcare industry, such as hospitals and local governments. In order to speed up developments and grab the momentum in digital healthcare in China, Baidu also started to invest in ventures. In 2015 Baidu invested 10 million USD in Yihu.com, a Chinese hospital registration platform, and a B round investment in Quyiyuan.com, another Chinese hospital registration platform that connects directly to the hospital information system.

In 2013–2015, Baidu made seven investments in online education, encompassing language (HJclass), music (Tonara), and comprehensive online courses platform (InnoBuddy, wanxue.cn, SmartStudy.com). An important investment was in Chuanke.com, an online course sharing platform, similar to Coursera, but not connected to specific universities, but skills and exams oriented. Initially Baidu invested B round 10 million USD in 2013 but in 2014 they fully acquired the company. By now, this company has been renamed Baidu Chuanke and is Baidu's core online education platform.

Baidu entered the Internet finance sector slowly. In October 2013 Baidu launched the first wealth management product collaborating with Huaxia Fund. And in 2014 Baidu upgraded their third party payment product to Baidu Wallet. As their key payment product, 90 million users have used Baidu Wallet (September 2016). After this upgrade, Baidu's strategy for Internet finance became clear and includes three modules: 1) Baidu Wealth Management and Wallet for consumers; 2) Baidu Bangbangdai, SME loans; 3) Baidu Finance Cloud for financial institutions. Moreover, in 2016, Baidu partnered with China CITIC Bank to establish a new bank: Baixing Bank, directly competing with the other Internet banks: Alibaba's MYbank, Tencent's WeBank and Xiaomi's XinWang Bank.

Baidu has also been active in connecting search to service and following the popular trend of location based services in China. Notable services include Baidu Waimai (2014), a food delivery service; Baidu Nuomi (invested in 2013, acquired in 2014), a Chinese group buying service; Baidu Ticket (2013), online ticket agency; and Baidu Travel (2011), online travel agency. Figure 7.1 shows the business ecosystem of Baidu.

Of course, not all of Baidu's diversification initiatives went well. For instance, Baidu has been active in developing toolkits for Internet users such as a browser, Chinese input system, virus scanner and media player. However, these products have not really succeeded in the market. Baidu has experimented with new products and technologies. An interesting example is the story of the Baidu Smart Chopsticks.

FIGURE 7.1 Baidu ecosystem (selected examples)

Source: authors' own figure.

On April 1, 2014, Baidu widely announced that they had developed magical smart chopsticks that could test the quality of your food, playing into the food safety concerns of many Chinese citizens. However, being April 1st, it was in fact a Fool's Day's joke and Baidu by no means had this product ready. Nevertheless, netizens were very excited about this announcement and it even reached international news and conferences. Orders for these imagined chopsticks flowed in and Baidu had no choice but to develop this product. By September 2014 they launched a simple version of the smart chopsticks that could measure and test the oil temperature and quality, beverage and water PH value and sweetness of fruits. A serious joke became an actual product. The product did not really succeed in the market, in part because the product was relatively expensive. Nevertheless, it shows Baidu's willingness to experiment and the role of users in developing new products.

7.2.5 Internationalizing Baidu's ecosystem

The first attempt to internationalize Baidu was in 2006, when the Baidu Japan project was initiated. In January 2008, Baidu.jp went online at a time when the top two search engines in Japan, Yahoo! and Google, already took an 80% market share. The development and performance of the new search engine was not clear, however; the fact it closed down in 2015 indicated that it was not a big success.

During the next years, Baidu has also entered other emerging countries such as Brazil, Egypt, Indonesia and Thailand. For instance, Baidu started a collaboration with Orange Egypt, a French telecom provider, and they launched their mobile Internet explorer. Despite the effort Baidu made, its revenue from outside of China was less than 1% in 2014 and Baidu is hardly considered to be a real international company.

However, Li Yanhong repeated his ambition on many occasions. In 2015 Baidu hired Hu Yong, the former general manager of Huawei, Brazil, to lead the overseas business.

First, Baidu has established seven overseas branches in Brazil, India, Thailand, Indonesia, Japan, Egypt and the USA, and hired over 1,000 employees (half of them are local) with a strategic focus on promoting mobile software tools to attract local users. Software tools such as DU Battery Saver, DU Speed Booster, ES File, Mobo Market, and Simeji (a Japanese input system) has been used in over 200 countries and regions with about 260 million monthly active users by the end of 2015. After accumulating big amount of users of its software tools, Baidu started to expand its businesses and generate revenue gradually.

Second, Baidu has also been investing in ventures abroad since 2013, reaching a percentage of overseas investments of total investment of 17%. In terms of geographic distribution, about half were in USA, while investments in the other countries such as Israel, Singapore, Japan and Finland were more or less equally distributed; see Figure 7.2. In terms of sectoral distribution, the two sectors with the most investment are LBS and culture and entertainment. Moreover, the investment sizes range from seed investment to 600 million USD (the strategic investments in Uber). We also see that over 30% of its overseas investments were acquisition, which is combined with further actions. For instance, Baidu acquired Brazilian group buying website Peixe Urbano and helped this company to grow its local market share to 70%, outcompeting Groupon to be the No. 1 group buying company in Brazil.

2016 was a good year for Baidu's internationalization. Its overseas revenue has increased five times above the corresponding period of last year. In particular, Baidu's users in the USA and Europe also grew significantly from 8% to over 30% of its global users (Wallstreet China, 2016). No doubt, in the future Baidu will keep internationalizing, towards a global ecosystem with software tools, services, content and information search and data.

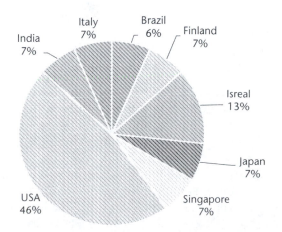

FIGURE 7.2 Baidu's overseas investments: geographic distribution (end 2016; # of deals)

Source: authors' own BATXL database.

7.3 The ecosystem of Tencent

Tencent is currently Asia's most valuable company and one of the world's largest Internet companies with a focus on social communication. Tencent's most popular instant messaging service WeChat has over 840 million active monthly users in China and over 100 million estimated abroad (2016) according to Tencent's financial reports. The total revenues of Tencent in 2015 reached 16 billion USD (year-to-year growth of 30%) with a net profit of 4.4 billion USD. Tencent's market capitalization is an estimated 230 billion USD (January 2017). Over the last decade Tencent has diversified into culture and entertainment (gaming), cloud, digital healthcare, Internet finance and is highly active in overseas investments and acquisitions. In 2007 and 2014 *Time* magazine called founder Ma Huateng one of the world's most influential people.

7.3.1 Origin of Tencent: Ma Huateng

Born in 1971, Ma Huateng is from Shantou City, Guangdong province. He studied computer science engineering in Shenzhen University and graduated in 1993 with a bachelor's degree. After graduation he worked for Runxun Telecom as a R&D engineer until founding Tencent with his four classmates: Zhang Zhidong, Xu Chenye, Chen Yidan and Zeng Liqing. His original idea for Tencent (founded in 1998) was to build an Internet pager system, by which you can send information via the Internet to your pager. China Telecom Guangdong had organized a bidding for such a system and Ma Huateng planned to develop and sell this system to them. Eventually they succeeded in the product development but failed to get the business from China Telecom. At that moment, they decided to run the product themselves. Nevertheless, the declining market for pagers did not show much promise. So, they went on to develop a Chinese instant messaging solution, later dubbed OICQ, or Open ICQ.

7.3.2 Beginning of an ecosystem: The core of serving social communication needs

Inspired by ICQ, the world's first Internet instant messaging service, founded in 1996 by an Israeli company, many Chinese companies were developing a similar product such as Sina Pager and PICQ. However, OICQ was simpler and more user friendly than their competitors. Moreover, the product was small in size and easy to download which was very crucial for users considering the limited Internet speed and costly bandwidth. Within a year they accumulated five million registered users. It is noteworthy that from the beginning Tencent's philosophy was on user oriented design and simplicity, which is still seen in the current version of their products. In the face of the America Online (AOL) lawsuit in 2000, they decided to change the name from OICQ to QQ. South African media and technology company Naspers purchased a 46% share of Tencent in 2001. The Chinese bank ICBC would later invest in Naspers and it is often misunderstood that Tencent is therefore a state-owned company.

Since 2009 Tencent started to move their products to mobile platforms. In 2011 Xiaomi, a smartphone producer founded in 2010, see Chapter 8, launched a mobile instant messenger called MiChat. Tencent had to do something or would lose its market advantage to a newcomer. Of course, it would have been possible to move their online instant messaging chat service QQ to mobile platforms. However, they decided to launch a new product, which can perfectly meet the social and communication needs in the mobile era, not just a modified version of last generation PC product. In fact, there was a team led by Zhang Xiaolong, the founder of Foxmail, one of the most talented programmers in China, that focused on developing QQ mailbox originally, and later proactively came out with a new product: WeChat. This particular team had time, was in fact not very busy, making it possible to develop a radically new product. It is interesting to know that Zhang Xiaolong's team was not the only team in Tencent working on the new mobile product development. For instance, there was another new product development team that came up with a new product Q Message, which never showed up in the market. WeChat was launched in 2011, a little later than MiChat, but Tencent's experience and resources were sufficient to quickly outcompete MiChat. By 2016 over 800 million people worldwide use WeChat, either the Chinese version (650 million users) or the English version (150 million users). QQ at this stage has still over 860 million users. WeChat's functions are widespread and integrates Friend Circle social sharing (April 2012), WeChat Public Platform (July 2012), WeChat Pay (August 2013), WeChat Wallet (January 2014) and a variety of location based services such as buying movie tickets, booking taxis, etc. (December 2014). In April 2016, Tencent launched an enterprise version of WeChat, which is positioned as a social productivity tool.

7.3.3 Early expansion beyond the core: Social and gaming

In 2003, Tencent released its own portal QQ.com and made forays into the online games market in order to expand the business portfolio. Extending their revenue model (see overview in Table 7.1), Tencent started to sell membership services

TABLE 7.1 Evolution of Tencent's revenue model

	Revenue stream of Tencent
1998–2005	Advertising and premium users of QQ, who pay monthly fees to receive added extras
2005–2008	Charging for use of QQ mobile, its cellular value-added service, and licensing its iconic penguin character, which could be found on all kinds of snack food, toys and clothing in China
2008–2011	Tencent was seeing profit growth from the sale of virtual goods in QQ and games, via Tencent's online currency, Q Coins
2011–now	Diversified income from own businesses as well as strategic investments

such as virtual goods in QQ. By 2004, Tencent became the largest Chinese instant messaging service (holding 74% of the market). Also, they launched an online gaming platform in the same year, more or less fueled by the Hong Kong IPO. By 2016 Tencent is the largest online gaming company in revenues (Forbes, 2016). Tencent's online gaming platform started selling virtual goods like virtual weapons as well as emoticons and ringtones, which later became Tencent's largest revenue stream. The gaming platform and portal were all connected to the QQ service and formed the core of Tencent's emerging ecosystem. In 2005 Tencent further strengthened the core by launching QQ Zone, which is an online space for the user to share their pictures and has a daily number of uploads of over one million pictures in 2016. In the years up to 2009, Tencent kept improving and launching new services, mostly games. According to observers, Tencent's reputation was not very good in this period; in fact, they were often considered to be a copycat in China by Chinese firms, especially gaming companies. Whenever Tencent saw good or interesting game concepts, they would quickly follow and launch in their large user base. Only in later years, they changed their strategy from closed to open, and invested in a lot of other gaming companies, domestic and abroad.

7.3.4 Growth by related diversification: Innovation, incubation, investment

Tencent's growth strategy changed to diversification into related sectors in 2011. Tencent employed three mechanisms to diversify into different sectors successfully. First of all, Tencent has initiated several innovative products and services. These are developed mostly by Tencent itself and focus on new product development. As we have seen with the development of WeChat, Tencent is adept at developing new products with an approach that allows parallel product development. Second, Tencent has invested significantly in new companies and technologies. As we will see in Chapter 9, Tencent has the most proactive diversification by investment strategy; over 200 companies in a wide variety of sectors and phases joined the Tencent business ecosystem. Third, Tencent has an incubation strategy called 'Double Hundred Plan', initiated in January 2015. The plan aims to invest 10 billion RMB by 2018 to support 100 start-ups in mobile Internet, including smart hardware. Besides the plan, Tencent already initiated Entrepreneurship Bases in 2013. By 2017 they had over 20 different locations all over China. Nevertheless, Tencent's diversification is predominantly fueled by investment.

According to observers, five business areas stand out: ecommerce, digital healthcare, culture and entertainment, Internet finance and LBS. These new cores are developed by innovation, incubation and investment.

The first diversification beyond the core was the founding of ecommerce Paipai in order to compete with Alibaba in 2005. Tencent became a strategic investor in JD, which is the largest self-operated B2C ecommerce platform in China. Following an Amazon model of keeping stock of goods sold, JD is probably the only threatening competitor of Alibaba's ecommerce. Nevertheless, Tencent never succeeded in becoming an ecommerce player themselves and Tencent's Paipai was integrated in JD and no longer exists independently.

A second crucial diversification is into digital healthcare. We can distinguish internal and external initiatives. Internally they have been active in online sales of medicine since 2012; they also launched WeChat smart hospital platform; Dr. Tang, a smart blood sugar device incubated in the company; and in 2016 they launched an app 'Tengai Doctor'. Externally, Tencent has invested in eight companies domestically, many in areas complementary to their own developed products. Products such as digital doctor community (e.g. Dingxiangyuan) and hospital process optimization (e.g. Guahaowang). Moreover, they have invested in nine companies overseas in digital healthcare: Circle Medical, Watsi, CliniCloud, HomeHero, Tute Genomics, CloudMedx, Scanadu and Tissue Analytics in the USA, Practo in India. Unlike Alibaba, who is more active in medicine ecommerce, Tencent is focusing on data, connectivity and international leads. Besides their recent investments, Tencent has also established collaborations with hospitals, government, pharmaceutical companies and doctor communities.

Closer to its roots, Tencent has been diversifying in culture and entertainment sectors. Similar to rivals Baidu and Alibaba, Tencent sees the vast opportunity of the emerging entertainment industry in China. Gaming is part of their own initiatives in entertainment since 2005 which also helps Tencent to monetize the large user base. They have invested in 56 gaming companies, including 29 overseas. Besides gaming, another notable success is QQ Music which recently merged with the China Music Corp. and their two popular streaming services, Kugou and Kuwo. Tencent now has the largest streaming music platform of China. At the end of 2016, Tencent announced the Entertainment Quotient Plan (EQ Plan), an initiative that makes ways for third party online content creators on their QQ social platform. Lastly, Tencent Video is one of the leading online video streaming sites that offers a wide range of licensed and original content. In 2015 Tencent established two film and TV drama companies, Tencent Pictures and Penguin Pictures.

Internet finance is Tencent's other new business. The first online payment tool Tenpay (in Chinese: Caifutong) was launched in 2005, now boasting about five million monthly active users (Big Data Research, 2016). Together with Alibaba and Pingan, Tencent established the first Internet insurance company Zhongan Insurance in 2013 (see Section 5.3.4). QQ Wallet (2014) and WeChat Pay (2013) are currently their two leading online payment services. Licaitong was established in 2014 for wealth management services while Zixuangu was launched in 2015 for stock investment and management. Similar to Alibaba and Baidu, at the end of 2014 Tencent co-founded a new Internet bank 'WeBank' and Tencent also launched their own individual credit management service, directly competing with Alibaba's. All in all, we can see the company has been quickly building up an ecosystem of Internet finance businesses in less than three years.

Last but not least, Tencent has been an active investor in LBS companies; many of which are top unicorns in China. For instance, a 350 million USD investment in Ele.me together with JD and other partners (2015); several investment rounds in

Didi Chuxing since 2013; and obtaining 20% of Dianping, the leading restaurant review and LBS platform (2014). In total Tencent invested in 25 companies in the LBS sector, which is led by a young generation of change makers in China. Tencent plays a significant role in fuelling these ventures. An impressive example is the case of Ele.me: it is a food delivery venture founded by several Shanghai Jiaotong University students that combines a Taobao-like marketplace with a full blown logistics system, boasting their own 12,000 employee strong delivery force, presence in over 700 Chinese cities, with 180,000 connected restaurants and five million daily orders (NetEase, 2016). Altogether Tencent built up a significant business ecosystem around a core of social communication services, as illustrated in Figure 7.3.

7.3.5 Internationalizing Tencent's ecosystem

Tencent has announced a further and deeper internationalization of their products and services. Tencent's overseas involvement consists of four aspects: 1) investment; 2) gaming; 3) WeChat; 4) others, such as cloud and music greenfield initiatives (Sohu, 2015).

First, Tencent is an active international investor, in part to build up an overseas ecosystem of ventures and supporting or complementary services. In fact, Tencent was the most active investor in overseas investment with 28% of its investments outside China, compared to Alibaba 23%, Baidu 17%. The most well-known overseas investments include Snapchat, Riot Games and Lyft. Tencent's overseas investments started with acquiring a Korean game company GoPets in 2005. As of today, Tencent invested in about 79 companies abroad, predominantly in the USA (67%); see Figure 7.4. The target fields reflect Tencent's core strategic

FIGURE 7.3 Tencent ecosystem (selected examples in outer layer)

Source: authors' own figure.

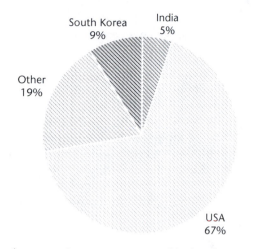

FIGURE 7.4   Tencent's overseas investments: geographic distribution (end 2016; # of deals)

Source: authors' own BATXL database.

directions and the diversification strategy mentioned in Section 7.2.4: gaming, social network services and healthcare are the top three sectors. The healthcare investment, on the other hand, illustrates that Tencent wants to explore advanced digital healthcare technology and new business models abroad. Moreover, Tencent has been an active investor all across the range of investment rounds, from seed investment to full acquisition with a clear early stage focus. The pre A and A round together are over 40%.

Looking for overseas targets, Tencent appears to co-invest with international VC funds such as the six projects co-invested with American VC SV Angel and another five projects co-invested with Anderson Horowitz. Moreover, the collaboration with overseas VCs intensified with the investment by Tencent in Digital Sky Technologies (DST) in 2010, a Russian Internet group which successfully invested Zynga, Facebook, JD and Alibaba.

Second, Tencent has been active in internationalizing their gaming business. They followed two approaches: import and export. They both import famous foreign games for the Chinese market and import successful foreign intellectual property to co-develop new games. In many cases, they import from and collaborate with the companies that they invested. Then, regarding export, they want to develop games for the overseas markets. Although it is still in the early phase, Tencent did make many efforts, such as invested in GluMobile, a USA game distributor and partnered with local game producers and distributors in Taiwan and South Korea.

Thirdly, internationalizing WeChat is a strategic focus that cannot be ignored. In 2012 they started to promote WeChat and later in 2015 WeChat Pay in Hong Kong. In Singapore they collaborated with a local taxi hailing app, EasyTaxi, to approach new users. In Indonesia they have a joint venture with a large local media company, PT Global Media, and already embedded in local Chinese communities. In South Africa, they have a joint venture with Naspers, promoting all kinds of services, including payment. In Europe, they cannot outcompete Whatsapp but nevertheless announced rapid user growth in Spain and Italy. In the USA they established a local branch in 2013 and heavily promoted with a subsidy commission approach and hired cultural ambassador, sport star Messi. The current user base abroad is over 270 million and these users are not only the overseas Chinese community but also foreign residents, especially those that have some sort of connection to China. However, the strong competition in combination with a lack of complementary services and infrastructure such as connected banks, utilities, restaurants, taxis, to name a few in foreign developed countries, makes that WeChat is mostly used as an instant messenger rather than the entry into Tencent's ecosystem of service offerings.

Lastly, besides the core of the service, Tencent has been active in other ways as well. In 2014 Tencent launched a music streaming service only available overseas: Joox.com. In 2015 Tencent has opened data centres in Hong Kong and the USA and revealed it will invest 1.57 billion USD over the next five years to boost a multinational cloud computing operation similar to Alibaba across North America, Hong Kong and China.

7.4 Concluding remarks

The business ecosystems of Baidu and Tencent have developed at great speed and with large diversity. While Baidu and Tencent are predominantly software focused ecosystems, similar to Alibaba's, they have also diversified widely into traditional and emerging sectors. While the case descriptions of the business ecosystems indicate certain similarities and differences, a detailed comparative analysis will follow in Chapter 9 to identify specific common features of Chinese business ecosystems, differences between business ecosystems, and to explore the dominant growth strategies of investment and internationalization across the cases. The following chapter will discuss the business ecosystems of Xiaomi and LeEco, newcomers and different in the way that they have a stronger hardware focus than BAT.

References

Baidu, 2016. *Baidu financial reports 2016*, Beijing, Baidu. Available at: http://ir.baidu.com/phoenix.zhtml?c=188488&p=irol-reportsannual. Accessed 22/02/2017.

Big Data Research, 2016. 2016 Nian 7 yue zhi fu lei APP yong hu jian ce bao gao [Payment APP user monitoring report in July 2016]. Available at http://www.bigdata-research.cn/content/201609/336.html. Accessed 22/02/2017 [in Chinese].

Forbes, 2016. *Tencent's winning game strategy*. Available at: https://www.forbes.com/sites/panosmourdoukoutas/2016/03/06/tencents-winning-game-strategy/#1262c337d16c. Accessed 22/02/2017.

NetEase, 2016. E le me xuan bu ri ding dan liang po 500 wan [Ele.me announced their daily orders are over five million]. Available at: http://tech.163.com/16/0607/23/BP0ARJVG00097U7R.html. Accessed 22/02/2017 [in Chinese].

Niubb, 2015. Bai du chuang ye shi [Baidu entrepreneurship history]. Available at: http://www.niubb.net/a/2015/11-06/899985.html. Accessed 22/01/2017 [in Chinese].

Sohu, 2015. Jie mi teng xun quan qiu hua de si da bu ju [Tencent's our globalization approaches exposed]. Available at: http://mt.sohu.com/20151226/n432673721.shtml. Accessed 22/02/2017 [in Chinese].

Tencent, 2016. *Tencent financial reports 2016*, Shenzhen, Tencent. Available at: https://www.tencent.com/en-us/investor.html. Accessed 22/02/2017.

The New York Times, 2017. China gains on the US in the artificial intelligence arms race. Available at: https://www.nytimes.com/2017/02/03/technology/artificial-intelligence-china-united-states.html?smid=tw-share. Accessed 15/02/2017.

Wallstreet China, 2016. Shou ru nian zeng 5 bei, bai du guo ji hua shi zhe yang zuo dao de [Revenues increased fivefold, this is how Baidu internationalized]. Available at: http://wallstreetcn.com/node/260948. Access 22/02/2017 [in Chinese].

8

NEWCOMERS XIAOMI AND LEECO

8.1 Introduction

While Chapter 7 discussed the business ecosystems of Alibaba's early competitors Baidu and Tencent, this chapter discusses the business ecosystems of newcomers Xiaomi and LeEco. These two business ecosystems were formed later and are generally speaking at an earlier stage of development than BAT's ecosystems. Although Xiaomi's founding team consist of veteran entrepreneurs and professionals, the company is still relatively young. LeEco's core business started in 2004 but transformed into an ecosystem just recently. Xiaomi and LeEco have a hardware plus software approach in common. While Xiaomi is mostly developing a hardware ecosystem around consumer electronics, LeEco focuses on expanding the possibilities to view their digital content via screens and consoles, even up to digital window screens in driverless cars. Based on Chinese publications on Xiaomi and LeEco and our research as indicated in Sections 1.3–1.4, in this chapter we discuss how Xiaomi and LeEco build up their business ecosystems and in particular focus on their growth, way of diversifying and internationalization.

8.2 The ecosystem of Xiaomi

Xiaomi is a Chinese mobile Internet company focused on smart hardware and electronics. Within three years after launching their smartphone, Xiaomi bested Apple and became the number one smartphone seller in China in 2014. By 2016 Xiaomi has sold over 150 million smartphones and expanded their electronics portfolio to over 30 product categories, including six self-developed products categories and 24 invested product categories, such as air purifiers, TVs, earphones, wearables, self-balancing scooters and rice cookers. The total revenues of Xiaomi in 2015 reached 12.5 billion USD, up only 5% of 2014 (MyDrivers, 2016). However, it is noteworthy that Xiaomi's exponential growth from 2010–2014 was at a compound average annual rate of 265%. Moreover, Xiaomi is one of the most valuable Chinese unicorns with a market capitalization of 45 billion USD and No. 2 on the list of 50 Smartest Companies 2015 by *MIT Technology Review*. In April 2016, the founder Lei Jun was on the cover of *Wired* magazine claiming 'it's time to learn from China'.

8.2.1 Origin of Xiaomi: Lei Jun and his all-star team

The founder and chairman of Xiaomi, Lei Jun, was born in Xiantao City, Hubei Province, in 1969. He entered the computer science major of Wuhan University in 1987 and within two years he finished all the required courses and thesis. During his remaining time at the university he wrote several software programs applied in finance, encryption and antivirus and even became a local celebrity in the Wuhan Electronics Street. In his own words, he was inspired by the book Michael Swaine *Fire in the Valley: The Making of the Personal Computer* and Steve Jobs was his personal example at that time. In his last year of college, he started his first company with three classmates. Initially the company imitated the Chinese card for transforming an English computer system to Chinese language from Kingsoft, a leading Chinese software company. However, they were outcompeted and went bankrupt. He started working for Kingsoft in 1992 and within six years he became the CEO of the company, working there until 2007, leading the company's IPO. In his years at Kingsoft he co-founded Joyo.com (2000), an online bookstore, which was sold to Amazon in 2004 for 75 million USD. After resigning at Kingsoft in 2007, Lei became a professional angel investor. He invested in dozens of companies such as Vancl.com (apparel ecommerce), YY (online audio video social platform, later listed on NASDAQ) and UCWeb (mobile browser and search, later acquired by Alibaba). In 2011 he founded Shunwei Capital, a professional VC fund, which invested about 50 companies by 2016. Despite his success in investment field, Lei Jun's recent major endeavour is Xiaomi, which was established in April 2010.

Together with six senior professionals and two angel investors (Morningside and Qiming Ventures), Lei Jun co-founded Xiaomi in Beijing. Lei Jun was not the only one with significant entrepreneurial experience: Lin Bin, former Google China Engineering Research Academy vice dean; Zhou Guangping, former Motorola Beijing R&D Center senior director; Liu De, former Beijing Science & Technology University Industrial Design department head; Li Wanqiang, former Kingsoft iCiba general manager; Huang Jiangji, former Microsoft China Engineering Academy development director; and Hong Feng, former Google China senior product manager. With this star team, Xiaomi set out to disrupt the smartphone market and build a 'bamboo forest' of fast growing hardware companies.

8.2.2 Beginning of an ecosystem: MIUI OS and Internet thinking

Xiaomi first launched their MIUI, which is an Android-based OS for smartphones, in August 2010. Three months later they further launched MiChat, the most pioneering smartphone chat tool in their OS. At that time the broader audience actually did not know or realize who developed MIUI. The company wanted to test the market without pulling big names. The goal was to create a user friendly OS by means of iterated development with quick updates based on the feedback of the users and open source developers community. One year after the launch, Xiaomi MIUI gained a following of half a million fans. Interestingly, MIUI fans emerged in 24 countries and volunteered to translate to their local languages. This first group of fans has been crucial for Xiaomi as they created a strong and large first loyal user base before launching any commercial product. This has been a break with the traditional smartphone industry and business approach of traditional marketing. Later Lei Jun would adopt the term 'Internet thinking' and 'fans marketing' to describe this approach.

According to Lei Jun, Internet Thinking has four concepts: focus, perfection, word of mouth, quick. Focus refers to limited product versions; perfection refers to building the product beyond the customer's expectation; word of mouth refers to making use of social media and earned media rather than paid media; 'quick' refers to rapid market introduction and in particular quick response to market requirements and iterations in product development. The concept of Internet Thinking has been adopted by other traditional industry giants. For instance, Lenovo's Liu Chuanzhi described it as the interactive feature of Internet Thinking, together with cloud computing and big data that allows manufacturers to directly understand their customer needs. Also, Haier's Zhang Ruimin, famous for disruptive ideas on innovation, adopted the concept and highlights that innovation should be user centred instead of product centred, allowing interaction with customers to understand their real needs and make sure they will buy your new products. Fans marketing and iterated product development are the core of Xiaomi's business model, as we will see with the products developed in the coming years.

8.2.3 Own product development: In search of the perfect business model

Building a smartphone is not an easy task, especially with Lei Jun's focus on a light asset business model, i.e. in-house software R&D and product design but no core hardware R&D, key components, production and delivery all outsourced. Therefore, before launching the first smartphone, Xiaomi needed to build a supply chain system that would support his business model. It turned out to become one of the strategic advantages of Xiaomi. In the beginning Xiaomi was refused by 85 of the top 100 smartphone component suppliers. In the first half year of 2011 the co-founders had over a 1,000 meetings with potential suppliers. Even just two weeks after the Fukuyama nuclear disaster, Lei Jun and his team still flew to Sharp to discuss supply agreements. After great effort, they finally got contracts with suppliers similar to Samsung's and Apple's, such as Qualcomm, Sony, Sharp and O-Film. Having settled the supplier problem and with half a million MIUI fans, in August 2011, Xiaomi launched their first smartphone. In the first four months they sold 300,000 smartphones. With subsequent new releases they reached seven million unit sales in 2012, in 2013 reaching 19 million and reaching a peak in 2014 with over 60 million smartphones, reaching No. 1 market position in China (IHS Technology, 2015).

Since their establishment, Xiaomi launched the Xiaomi series, Red Rice series and Note series, totalling over 20 versions. The Xiaomi Youth launched in May 2012 is a good example of how Xiaomi employed the 'fans marketing' model. Two months before the official launch date, the company posted a topic called '150 grams youth' in Weibo (Chinese Twitter). Under this topic they shared many nostalgic drawings reminding young people of their undergraduate time and campus life. All kinds of guesswork came into play: What does '150 grams' mean? For boys it may be a camera or gaming console; for girls it may be a scale. They even recorded a micro movie called 'Our 150 grams youth', starring the seven co-founders in animated style published in Youku (Chinese YouTube). On the launch day they disclosed the puzzle's answer and it was the weight of the Xiaomi's new smartphone Youth; the news posted in Weibo was forwarded two million times in one day and as a result of the successful fans marketing, 150,000 phones were sold out within 11 minutes.

Following the initial success of the Xiaomi smartphone, the company started to look for its next success story. In the following period Xiaomi launched a Xiaomi Pad, Xiaomi Notebook, Xiaomi TV, Xiaomi TV Box and Xiaomi Router. In the course of developing these new products, Xiaomi also got more confident in their business model. Xiaomi's business model contains the following features:

- Fans marketing: using social media to promote the product by earned media rather than paid media. The result is a base of fans that follow the social media of Xiaomi and take active part in the Xiaomi community.
- Iterated software R&D and product design: using a new product development approach that focuses on getting prototypes on the market as soon as possible, i.e. with 'almost' good enough products, and actively involve the users in fine-tuning and updating the technology and design. The result is a product that is to a large extent co-developed by the community, i.e. closer to the market need, and with a more efficient R&D process.
- Online sales: using online sales channels and social media platforms instead of heavy asset retail shops and distributors. Considering the narrow target market of young engineering focused and tech savvy men, the online sales channel meets the expectations of this market. The result is a low cost sales channels that meet the demands of the initial target group of customers.
- Outsource components, production and delivery: using the best qualified suppliers for components and focus on integration and design rather than production and hardware R&D. The key competence of Xiaomi is business model, marketing and promotion and design, rather than manufacturing. The result is that they can deliver similar quality products without the investments in production and R&D.

It is interesting to note that in this phase the above business model has worked remarkably well. However, as we will see later, Xiaomi is not stubborn in keeping this business model and by 2017 Xiaomi, for instance, announced to also develop offline sales channels for the 3rd and 4th tier markets that are less tech savvy and prefer to buy offline rather than online; largely in response to emerging competitors Oppo and Vivo. Nevertheless, in 2012–2014 this business model fit well with their target market and the business conditions at that time. Having successfully developed this business model, Xiaomi was now looking for quicker ways to expand and diversify. Xiaomi developed a novel way of high speed diversification of their products.

8.2.4 Growth by diversification: Building a 'bamboo forest'

At the end of 2013 Xiaomi launched a new strategic initiative: building a Xiaomi ecosystem. In principle, they wanted to copy their successful business model to other products. However, instead of developing and designing the products themselves, as they had done before, they resorted to investing in other companies. The ambitious goal was to invest in 100 companies within five years (CBN, 2014). By the end of 2016 they claimed to invest in around 70 companies, ranging from smart lights, air purifiers, earphones, to rice cookers, remote controls, smart scales, suitcases and blood pressure cuffs (CBN, 2016). Figure 8.1 shows that Xiaomi has been investing predominantly in hardware ventures. Their diversification is at high speed and with large product variety, e.g. smart home, consumer electronics and personal transport. Moreover, each invested company got the 'Xiaomi makeover' with the Xiaomi brand, marketing, product design and development, supply chain and internal process management templates, indicating a strong incubating feature which is quite different from BATL. In fact, Xiaomi has left many incumbents in consumer electronics startled.

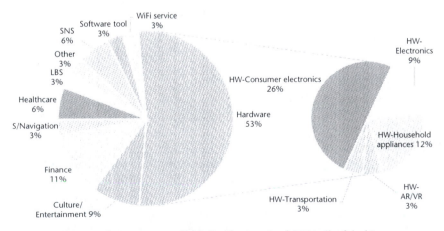

FIGURE 8.1 Xiaomi's investments: field distribution (end 2016; # of deals)

Source: authors' own BATXL database.

In the first year of their new strategy, Xiaomi mostly focused on incubating early stage projects. As an illustrative example, we take the air purifier, launched in December 2014. In fact, at that time Xiaomi saw a big market need for air purifiers but could not find a suitable producer in the market and then suggested Su Jun, the former associate professor of industrial design at North China University of Technology, to develop an air purifier and Xiaomi invested in the start-up. Within nine months the product was developed and launched with a killer price of 899 RMB, only one third of the average market price at that time.

In the second year, 2015, Xiaomi started to focus on more mature companies such as Ninebot, a leading Chinese self-balancing scooter producer. Xiaomi not only invested in the company, but also helped Ninebot acquire Segway and launch a new product with a killer price of 1,999 RMB. Xiaomi's product design, supply chain bargaining power and large user base allowed Ninebot to reduce the cost significantly. Altogether, so far the Xiaomi business model has proven successful in many of the invested products and companies and Xiaomi is building a comprehensive business ecosystem around the OS and smartphone core; see Figure 8.2.

8.2.5 Internationalizing Xiaomi's ecosystem

Xiaomi has been active in internationalizing. First of all, from the beginning the MIUI had fans all over the world. In 2013 Xiaomi entered Taiwan and Hong Kong and in 2014 entered Singapore, Malaysia, the Philippines, India and later Russia and Turkey. They also entered Brazil in 2015 but within one year already decided to exit the market. In the same year Huawei and ZTE also left the market, mainly due to local protectionism, taxes, and unpredictable and frequent regulatory changes. Second, in 2017 Xiaomi has been promoting their consumer electronics products in the USA during the Consumer Electronics Show (CES) in Las Vegas. They released their new products, the MIX smartphone, Xiaomi router and Xiaomi TV 4. Third, in an attempt to internationalize the company, Xiaomi attracted Hugo

FIGURE 8.2   Xiaomi ecosystem (selected examples in outer layer)

Source: authors' own figure.

Barra, the former Google Android head, to lead their international department. His first moves were to enter the Indian market and did so with reasonable success, leading up to 1 billion USD revenues of sales with 6.5 million phone sales in 2016. Nevertheless, the market share of Xiaomi's overseas business of Chinese overseas smartphone producers is only ranked No. 7. Mr. Barra left the company in January 2017.

The company is currently not investing overseas; actually, Xiaomi only invested in Pebbles Interfaces, an Israeli technology company in 2013, which was acquired by Facebook in 2015. Moreover Xiaomi is also not significantly expanding into new markets. An important reason for Xiaomi's domestic focus is the intellectual property challenges faced abroad. For instance, the lawsuit by Ericsson in India in 2013 led to a temporary ban on Xiaomi smartphones' import. Nevertheless, Xiaomi's second attempt in 2015–2016 was successful and it is noteworthy that Ratan Tata of the Tata Group acquired a stake in Xiaomi after the initial success in India. In June 2016 Xiaomi announced it had acquired over 1,500 patents from Microsoft, indicating they are building up an IP basis, and broadening their partnership with Microsoft (Microsoft, 2016). Nevertheless, Lei Jun announced that 2017 will be an important year for Xiaomi's internationalization and Xiaomi has to overcome the difficulties.

8.3 The ecosystem of LeEco

LeTV (later rebranded LeEco in 2016) is China's first online video platform with over a decade of experience in video sharing, production and distribution. With over 76 million users domestically, it is one of the most successful online video platforms in China. The total revenues of LeEco's listed part, LeTV are close to 2 billion USD in 2015 with an annual growth of 90% and market capitalization of 11 billion USD (February 1, 2017) while LeEco also boasts four unicorns in its ecosystem: LeSports, LeCloud, LePictures and LeMobile. Moreover, LeEco is the only company of the five in this book that is daring to directly enter the USA market with a deep dive, as we will discuss in Chapter 9.

8.3.1 Origin of LeEco: Jia Yueting

Jia Yueting, was born in 1973, Xiangfen County, Shaanxi province. He studied in Shaanxi Finance and Taxation Specialized School, majoring in accounting and computer science as a double major. Upon graduation he was appointed to Shaanxi Yuanqu County Tax Office as a computer administrator. In less than one year he quit his job and started his first venture in training education. In 2002 he founded Shaanxi Xibeier Telecom Science & Technology and supplied accessories to base stations of China Unicom. Mr. Jia made his first capital with this venture. Then in 2004 he decided to step into online video service and founded LeEco in Beijing, to be followed by the launch of his online video website LeTV.com.

Jia Yueting's personality and business philosophy is not afraid of experimentation. He said, only if 99% of the people do not see the value in an opportunity, it may have the potential to become disruptive. This is also part of LeEco's business genes. The company started with an online video platform based on acquired intellectual property of films and TV dramas in a time that most of the other video platforms freely uploaded contents without legal permission. His later direct move into the USA market has also raised many eyebrows since even the 'big brothers' BAT had not yet succeeded. Let alone the entry into the electric and driverless car industry: while many would have expected a light asset approach similar to Xiaomi, Mr. Jia chose the heavy asset approach and is building car factories himself in the USA and in China.

8.3.2 Core of LeEco's ecosystem: Serving entertainment needs

LeTV.com went online in 2004; an online video platform with all the paid IP. At a time in China where piracy of music and video was at its high time, it was an unusual approach. LeTV.com was a website based video portal where online content included Chinese movies and Chinese TV series. Mr. Jia saw a specific opportunity in the increase of bandwidth and maturing of video decoding technology. The type of medium with which movies are shared and distributed has been moving from CD to DVD and Blue Ray, but soon there will be a pure digital release revolution. Chris Anderson's book *Free* was popular at that time and most Internet ventures were offering freemium services. Most other Internet companies thought that LeEco's business model was rather unusual, as it charged users instead of using the freemium model. In a way this showcases Mr. Jia's business approach: doing things different.

Two years after launching the web portal, LeEco started to collaborate with China Central Television (CCTV) and created a mobile TV service; i.e. watching CCTV broadcasts via phones. In 2007 LeEco launched their own software LeTV and were no longer dependent on websites but their own platform applications. With great success, they supported the live streaming of the Chinese Spring Festival Gala in 2007. Then in 2008, four years after their founding, LeEco got their first round of investment of 52 million RMB and was recognized by Deloitte as the No. 3 fastest growing high technology enterprise in China. Moreover, in the same year they started to offer online premium services such as exclusive premieres of TV series and realized simultaneous TV broadcasting, indicating LeEco's LeTV quickly became a real alternative for cable TV. By 2009, all of the content could be viewed on mobile terminals such as smartphones.

2010 was an important year for LeEco as they became the first domestically listed Internet video company in China. With the raised capital, LeEco started to diversify into content production and eventually hardware design and manufacturing and it took only a few years before it became a business ecosystem, with four global unicorns and a global business outlook. LeEco made a big technological leap in 2014, when all their content and services moved into the LeCloud, the newly established cloud computing and data processing company. In May 2016 LeCloud received a large investment of close to 1 billion RMB, currently also a unicorn valued venture. As part of LeEco's global expansion plan, LeCloud now covers 750 CDN network nodes across 60 countries and regions, providing service for over 100,000 enterprise users (LeCloud, 2016).

8.3.3 Diversification: From content to hardware

8.3.3.1 Content making: LePictures

In 2011 LePictures was established. Jia Yueting hired Zhang Zhao, previous CEO of Inlight Pictures, a successful domestic movie producer, to run LePictures. By 2012, LePictures already published six movies with box office sales of over 600 million RMB. Then, in search to boost their visibility and quality, in May 2013, Zhang Yimo, a famous movie director in China, became art director of LePictures. In the same year they also received the first round investment of 200 million RMB. With the rapid growth of their movies and box office sales, they received their B round investment in 2014 and later C round in 2015 with a valuation of 7 billion RMB (Sina, 2017). Besides developing LePictures, LeEco also acquired a movie making company Innotree (in Chinese: *Huaeryingshi*) in 2014. Another successful content venture in the ecosystem is LeSports, a spinoff of the original sports channel in LeTV, which also received a large investment with a valuation of 22 billion RMB in December 2016.

8.3.3.2 Hardware: three companies, three product groups (TV, smartphone and smart electronics)

Mr. Jia made an announcement that September 19, 2012, is the disruption day of LeEco and LeEco would not only enter into content production but also in making smart Internet TVs. By 2013 Leshi Zhixing, the new company for the TV business, released the long-planned SuperTV with self-developed OS EUI TV and a joint effort of Sharp, Qualcomm and Foxconn. Before they could launch the SuperTV, they had to develop software such as LeTV UI and LeStore; a Smart TV app collection which has over 2,000 apps – the store has also been pre-installed in smart TVs and set-top boxes by many local brands (launched in 2013). Mr. Jia predicts that TVs won't be TVs anymore but the computing centre and the Internet platform for families. Internet based service providers will be new market leaders, according to Mr. Jia. So far, Leshi Zhixin has sold over 10 million SuperTVs, becoming one of the largest Internet TV suppliers in China, following a 'low price for hardware plus subscription model'. Next to that LeEco also invested in TCL, the largest TV producer in China and Coolpad, a large Chinese smartphone producer. It is important to note that the listed LeTV has a majority controlling stake in LeTV Zhixing, although not part of the listed LeTV. In February 2017 LeEco sold a part of their TV business shares for over 100 million USD.

After successfully launching the SuperTV, LeEco had taste for more. Not unlike Xiaomi, LeEco copied the same approach to launching other branded hardware products. For instance, the company announced its new Le Superphone in April 2015, also establishing a new company LeMobile. Like other Android phone manufactures in China, LeMobile has also built its own operating system which is called EUI Mobile. Again, LeMobile poached top level industry executives from the phone industry, such as Meizu and Xiaomi. Already in 2015, the company sold 4 million phones and 15 million targeted in 2016. Other hardware products that follow the similar model include entertainment products such as LeVR, Le Smart Microphone, and blue tooth earphones and children electronics. Moreover, LeEco had established an online ecommerce platform LeMall in 2014, after starting selling TVs. On LeMall consumers can buy all their hardware products and also subscriptions for LeEco. Moreover, LeMall since 2016 also offers financial services via LeFinance, which was established in 2015. In 2015 LeEco established a new company, LeIE, to manage all the smart products, excluding the LeMobile's Le Superphone and Leshi Zhixin's SuperTV.

8.3.4 Growth by unrelated diversification: The LeSEE Plan

At the end of 2014, Mr. Jia announced the LeEco's Super Electric Ecosystem (LeSEE) Plan. The plan includes to build a super car and vertically integrate an Internet based smart transportation ecosystem and lifestyle. In January 2015, LeEco hired the former China general manager of Infiniti, a Japanese high end car brand, Lv Zhengyu, as the vice president of LeAutoLink. LeAutoLink is a newly established company (January 2015) and is not included in the listed part of LeEco. In the same month they launched EUI Auto, an OS for cars, boasting voice/touch/motion control, automatic navigation, group chat, music streaming, online radio/video, and roadside assistance services. LeEco hired the former general manager of Shanghai General Motors in the same year: Ding Lei. He became the co-founder and CEO of LeAutoLink. Furthermore, the company managed to hire Dr. Ni Kai, the top driverless car scientist, formerly Baidu senior scientist and Zhang Hailiang, the former general manager of SAIC Motor-Volkswagen Joint Venture. In March 2015 LeEco signed a strategic partnership with Beijing Automotive Group (BAIC) where BAIC will contribute their car manufacturing and R&D experience and LeEco will contribute their Internet technology, experience and capability. Within the same year they together launched an electric car EU260 with EUI Auto, LeEco's newly developed answer to CarPlay from Apple or Android Auto from Google or Baidu's CarLife; mobile phone connected car entertainment and support system, integrating other content providers and direct access to LeTV content.

In April 2015 LeEco and Aston Martin, a traditional high end car manufacturer in Europe, initiated an R&D project focusing on Internet vehicle technology. September of the same year, LeAutoLink invested 50 million RMB in Beijing based start-up DZ Technology, a company focusing on electric vehicle charging technology. In October 2015 LeAutoLink bought 70% shares of Yongche, China's first and also one of the largest online car ordering service providers. In January 2016, LeEco made a bold and contested strategic move into the American electric and autonomous car market by investing in Faraday Future with 1 billion USD for a car factory near Las Vegas. At the same time, together with Aston Martin, at the CES 2016 LeEco launched Rapide S which integrated EUI Auto.

In fact, LeEco has two distinct automotive initiatives; one with Aston Martin and one with Faraday Future. Aston Martin is a traditional car manufacturer and Faraday Future is a new start-up building electric cars. Their partnership with Aston Martin is to bring in the Internet of vehicle technology, autonomous drive technology as well as electrical power systems and transmission systems. The car was developed with an eye on the Chinese domestic market. Faraday is a new venture, with leadership coming from Tesla. LeEco is helping with the technology for the connectivity of cars and also work with them on autonomous driving. The market focus is a global one in direct competition with Tesla. Overall, these partnerships combine the perspective of a traditional car industry, and from the Internet technology perspective.

In March 2016 LeAutoLink signed a partnership with BYD and Dongfeng Motor. On the same day, they also launched two vehicle wearable devices: a video recorder (front window road monitoring) for the car and a remote control. Then, in April 2016 LeAutoLink launched their concept car LeSEE. In June LeEco signed a strategic collaboration agreement with GAG Group (Guangzhou car manufacturer) and UrTrust (car insurance company); together the three companies established a joint venture 'Dasheng Technology', which will focus on building car service platform for new and secondhand cars. Then in August 2016, the company announced it is going to build an automotive plant as well as an 'eco automotive experience' complex in China's Zhejiang Province with a total investment of 3 billion USD. According to the plan, all vehicles used in the 'automotive eco-town' will be electric, shared and driven autonomously. In addition, LeEco will also use content resources, such as music, sports and film in the town.

By now, LeAutoLink already includes activities such as smart Internet electric car R&D, manufacturing, sales, Internet of vehicles, smart driving, charging solutions, car sharing, basically establishing a whole value chain. The team of the company already has 750 employees, located in Beijing, Silicon Valley, Los Angeles and Germany. External investors see the potential in this ambitious plan. In August, 50 million USD was invested by China's Fortune 50 private company Macrolink and in September a second round of around 1 billion USD by several investors such as Lenovo Capital and Shenzhen Capital Group. Then, in January 2017 LeEco announced a partnership with their strategic investor Sunac China who invested 2.4 billion USD. Altogether LeEco has been developing a complex business ecosystem that not only focuses on the core of entertainment and video platform services but has developed new nodes, new sub-ecosystems in hardware consumer electronics and automotive, as illustrated in Figure 8.3. The hardware sub-ecosystem appears to follow a Xiaomi-like model of new product development but with one crucial difference: the companies are not invested and incubated but developed by LeEco.

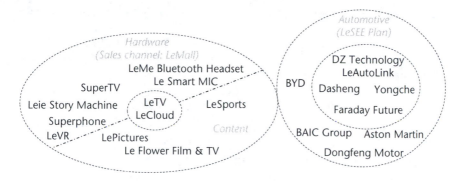

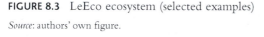

FIGURE 8.3   LeEco ecosystem (selected examples)

Source: authors' own figure.

8.3.5 Internationalizing LeEco's ecosystem: Conquering the USA?

LeEco's internationalization focuses on the USA market, in contrast to the broader and more diverse approaches of BAT and Xiaomi. First of all, LeMall is currently operating in the USA, India, Hong Kong and Russia. LeEco's big bet is the USA market. In the words of the VP for international strategy, LeEco's move into the USA is partly explained by ambition but also partly by the idea that experience in other markets will not matter much and only cost them precious time. In July 2016 LeEco announced to acquire Vizio, the second largest smart TV producer in the US, for around 2 billion USD. Under the deal LeEco will operate Vizio as a subsidiary, taking responsibility for the hardware business as well as their smart TV ecosystem.

On the 19th of October 2016, LeEco made their official debut into the US market. According to speech made by Jia Yueting in San Francisco, LeEco would begin selling their smartphones and SuperTVs from November 2016. Along with their main products, TVs (with offices already in Seattle and San Diego) and smartphones, they have also presented streaming service. Within one month, LeMall started their promotional activities in the USA. Furthermore, LeEco announced a strategic collaboration with AT&T in November 2016. AT&T is internationalizing and probably is going to leverage LeEco for entering the Chinese market. This collaboration is on top of the collaborations with BestBuy and Amazon. Also, LeCloud has had a USA subsidiary since January 2016. Moreover, LeCloud has a global strategic collaboration with Dell and Ericsson. Alltogether, LeEco's vested interests in the USA are significant.

The internationalization and diversification has also led to serious challenges for LeEco. In particular, as announced by the founder in November 2016, the non-listed companies of LeEco face cash flow problems (Forbes, 2016). Nevertheless, the company appears to be open to share such difficulties with the public and Mr. Jia is willing to discuss their challenges. And, according to observers, Jia Yueting is extremely resourceful in finding solutions. One week after announcing cash flow problems, he announced that he had raised 600 million USD for their car business.

8.4 Concluding remarks

The business ecosystems of Xiaomi and LeEco have developed at great speed and with large diversity. While Baidu and Tencent are predominantly software focused ecosystems, Xiaomi and LeEco have become mostly hardware focused ecosystems. While the case descriptions of the four business ecosystems indicate certain similarities and differences, a detailed comparative analysis will follow in Chapter 9 to identify specific common features of Chinese business ecosystems and differences between business ecosystems, and to explore the dominant growth strategies of investment and internationalization across the five cases.

References

CBN, 2014. Lei jun yu 5 nian tou zi 100 jia gong si [Lei Jun will invest 100 companies]. Available at: http://tech.sina.com.cn/i/2014-11-17/01149796114.shtml. Accessed 22/12/2016 [in Chinese]

CBN, 2016. Xiao mi shai sheng tai lian cheng ji dan [Xiaomi discloses the eco-chain report card]. Available at: http://tech.hexun.com/2016–03-30/183034025.html. Accessed 22/12/2016 [in Chinese]

Forbes, 2016. LeEco CEO Jia Yueting says company overstretched In letter to employees. Available at: https://www.forbes.com/sites/tychodefeijter/2016/11/07/leecos-ceo-jia-yueting-says-company-overstretched-in-letter-to-employees/#45a1eeb827e6. Accessed 12/12/2016

IHS Technology, 2015. 2014 nian zhong guo shi chang zhi neng shou ji xiao liang [Smartphone sales of Chinese market in 2014]. Available at: http://tech.hexun.com/2015-01-23/172683005.html. Accessed 22/12/2016 [in Chinese]

LeCloud, 2016. Yun xin wen zhu tui chuan tong mei ti gai ge le shi yun you bie chu da zhao [Cloud new reform and LeCloud's expansion]. Availabe at: http://www.lecloud.com/zh-cn/news/2016/08/22/375.html. Accessed 30/12/2016 [in Chinese]

LeTV, 2016. *LeTV Financial Reports 2016*, Beijing, LeTV. Available at: http://www.cninfo.com.cn/cninfo-new/fulltextSearch?code=&notautosubmit=&keyWord=300104. Accessed 22/02/2017 [in Chinese]

Microsoft, 2016. Microsoft and Xiaomi expand partnership to bring productivity services to millions of devices and customers. Available at: https://news.microsoft.com/2016/05/31/microsoft-and-xiaomi-expand-partnership-to-bring-productivity-services-to-millions-of-devices-and-customers/#5wmB4Zt7t5z2AFU6.99. Accessed 22/02/2017

MyDrivers, 2016. Xiao mi 2015 nian ying shou, shou ji zong xiao liang bao guang [Xiaomi discloses 2015 revenue and smartphone sales]. Available at: http://news.mydrivers.com/1/483/483724.htm. Accessed 22/12/2016 [in Chinese]

Sina, 2017. Le shi ying ye gu zhi xia tiao [LePictures' valuation goes down]. Available at: http://finance.sina.com.cn/roll/2017-01-15/doc-ifxzqhka3100765.shtml. Accessed 22/02/2017 [in Chinese]

9

COMPARING CHINESE BUSINESS ECOSYSTEMS

9.1 Introduction

While BATXL all fostered business ecosystems and enjoyed rapid growth and diversification into a variety of sectors, the assessment of their transformation in Chapters 7 and 8 suggest that they do not only share common features. In fact, the growth approaches and speed of transformation appear to diverge. What are the differences between the business ecosystems of BATXL? Can we identify specific types of business ecosystems? Are the growth approaches of the business ecosystems diverging or converging? What are the investment approaches of BATXL and is there any difference? Moreover, considering that BATXL have many overlapping business activities, do they compete with each other as business ecosystems or in different ways? Lastly, given that all of the business ecosystems are attempting to internationalize, do we find different patterns and strategies?

In this chapter we compare the business ecosystem of Alibaba to Baidu, Tencent, Xiaomi and LeEco. In what follows we compare the business ecosystems on the following aspects: founding, growth, ecosystem mechanism, innovation, incubation, investment, competition and internationalization. Section 9.2 provides a summary of our Alibaba case with key insights as to facilitate comparison with Baidu, Tencent, Xiaomi and LeEco. The founding, growth, mechanism, innovation and incubation of the business ecosystems will be discussed in Section 9.3. Considering the importance of investment by growth for BATXL, we will provide a detailed comparison in Section 9.4. Along the same lines, we will provide an assessment of competition in Section 9.5 and a detailed comparison of the internationalization of BATXL in Section 9.6. We conclude with a summary of insights in Section 9.7.

9.2 Alibaba case insights: Investment, incubation, innovation, internationalization

The continuous transformation of Alibaba's business ecosystem ensures an increasingly better satisfaction of customer needs and better fit into the changing business context. The case shows the strong and effective strategic renewal capability of Alibaba's business ecosystem. In a fast growing market with the middle class boom, the strong driving force of the digital technology, and an increasingly supportive regulatory environment, especially for equity investments, Alibaba grew fast. At the same time, Alibaba's business ecosystem is co-evolving with its context; for instance, Alibaba has played a significant role in defining industries such as ecommerce, Internet finance, digital healthcare and smart logistics.

Moreover, while the core of Alibaba's ecosystem was developed internally, the rapid growth and change of the business ecosystems was fuelled by a particular hybrid growth strategy: growth by investment, incubation and entrepreneurship, innovation and internationalization. First, the high investment activity has created a strong growth of the ecosystem and diversification of offerings: a wide diversity of emerging sectors and range of investments from pioneering start-ups to mature and public companies. Alibaba's strong financing capability, large cash flow, loan leverage and co-investment approach allowed Alibaba to invest rapidly and with large sums of investment. Alibaba follows an unique investment approach that is following high growth sectors rather than a planned approach such as of professional funds and corporate venturing. Second, Alibaba's business ecosystem is highly facilitative of entrepreneurial activities, within, across and outside of the ecosystem. Alibaba has proven to be a fertile ground for new ventures and hundreds of new CEOs. Third, the Ant Financial case illustrates how the business ecosystem has continuously innovated in response to market opportunity, restriction and competition. Fourth, Alibaba's international growth strategy has centred around four pillars, including import/export, greenfield, acquisition and partnership, while global ecommerce has been dominating. Alibaba follows a hybrid internationalization strategy with a variety of motives, ranging from scale to market and technology.

9.3 Diverging business ecosystems

9.3.1 Founding

The origins of the five ecosystems are very different, from focusing on commodity needs (Alibaba), information needs (Baidu), social communication needs (Tencent), to fans' needs (Xiaomi) and entertainment needs (LeEco). The difference of origin has significant strategic consequence. BATXL has different core competence and orientation which grew up out of their roots. The different orientation and core competence influenced their long term strategic directions. As we can see, especially in the case of BAT, but to a lesser extent also in XL, the business ecosystems centre on the original focus.

The lead founders of these five business ecosystems have different backgrounds and experiences. While Baidu's Li Yanhong is the only overseas returnee technologist and first time founder, Xiaomi's Lei Jun and LeEco's Jia Yueting are both local serial entrepreneurs with significant experiences, Alibaba's Ma Yun and Tencent's Ma Huateng are domestic first time entrepreneurs. Nevertheless, despite the seemingly less 'elite' background and experience of Ma Yun and Ma Huateng, their companies appear to have become the largest and, not the least, globally active.

BATXL also has very different founding teams. Although BAT's founding teams are all quite well known in China's Internet industry and even have specific nicknames, i.e. Alibaba's 18 *'arhats'*, Baidu's seven 'swordsman', Tencent's five 'tiger generals' the later development of the stories are not all as expected. The majority of Alibaba's original founders are still with Alibaba while the co-founders of Baidu all left, except Li Yanhong, and three of the five co-founders of Tencent left. However, Alibaba's founding team had to prove itself once more when in 2009 Jack Ma announced that all the co-founders had to resign and reapply for their 'job'. In this way, they attempted to guarantee the relevance of the co-founders but at the same time also send out a message to their employees that there's no such thing as an 'iron bowl'. In the case of Baidu, the earliest co-founder XU Yong, who came back with Li Yanhong from the USA, left Baidu right before Baidu's IPO while the others also left at an early stage. Observers suggest that Li Yanhong might want to protect his dominant position, especially considering Xu Yong's relatively large equity share at that time. Tencent's co-founders left at a relatively late stage. The earliest resignation, in 2007, was when Liu Chiping, an external professional manager, was appointed president of Tencent, and co-founder Zeng Liqing, who later became a well known angel investor, left. The recently established Xiaomi (2010) has not yet seen any of the all-star team co-founders leave the company. For LeEco, the story is somewhat different, as Jia Yueting has been the single heroic founder.

BATXL's starting capital has come from a variety of sources. In fact, BAT all received their initial funds from abroad. While this may appear surprising, in the early 2000s there was not much of a VC industry in China (see Chapter 3) and these companies had not much choice but to attract foreign investors. For Li Yanhong this was a rather unsurprising step, being a Sillicon Valley overseas returnee, but it turns out that Ma Yun was particularly adept at raising foreign funds. Then, Xiaomi was established about a decade later and by then the VC industry in China was already booming. Moreover, Xiaomi's founding team consisted of experienced entrepreneurs, let alone that Lei Jun has been running his own fund for years; therefore raising domestic capital was not difficult. In fact, they co-founded Xiaomi with two domestic VCs. The outlier in this story is Jia Yueting's LeEco: there's no evidence that LeEco raised any significant external capital in the early stage, except potentially private informal capital. Moreover, it is important to notice that LeEco is not Mr. Jia's first successful business and he most likely accumulated enough capital for his LeEco venture by himself. All in all, BATXL's early developments are rather diverging. The comparison of BATXL's founding is summarized in Table 9.1.

TABLE 9.1 Diverging business ecosystems of BATXL: founding

	Baidu	Alibaba	Tencent	Xiaomi	LeEco
Origin	Information needs	Commodity needs	Social communication needs	Fans needs	Entertainment needs
Lead founder experience	Li Yanhong: first time successful entrepreneur	Ma Yun: first time successful entrepreneur	Ma Huateng: first time successful entrepreneur	Lei Jun: serial entrepreneur	Jia Yueting: serial entrepreneur
Founding team	Co-founded by seven partners, six already left in a relative early stage	Co-founded by 18 partners, most of them still work in Alibaba	Co-founded by five partners, three left in a relative late stage	All-star team of seven experienced entrepreneurs, nobody left so far	Single 'hero' entrepreneur
Starting capital	Large seed fund from the USA	Large seed fund from the USA	Large seed fund from South Africa	Large seed fund from China	Entrepreneur's own capital accumulated by former ventures

9.3.2 Growth

Alibaba's growth phases are quite well defined by periods in time with first the building of an ecommerce ecosystem, extension of the ecommerce ecosystem and then related diversification into other sectors. However, Baidu's growth seems to simultaneously adopt multiple approaches in parallel. For instance, Baidu's complementary community services and vertical search started in 2008 and full scale diversification occurred in 2011, but in the later period we still see new offerings that are complementary rather than fully diversified. The other way around, the earliest diversification with Baidu Games was already in 2007. Tencent's growth is similar to Alibaba's, however with a distinctive dual core of the ecosystem: QQ (web core) and WeChat (mobile core). Before 2011, it mainly focused on developing its core QQ by launching complementary products or services like QQ.com (2003), QQ Game (2004) and QQ Zone (2005). In 2011, the other core, WeChat, grew up and together with its related constrained diversification in various fields such as such as web security, social network services, location based services, software tool and Internet finance. When looking at Xiaomi's development, we see a phased development where Xiaomi first tried out their business model with one product, smartphone, then early on diversified the business by extending with a handful of their self-developed products and in the final phase scaled up the application of their business model by investing in and incubating a whole range of companies. LeEco's development has moved away much further from the core of the ecosystem than BATX and all by its own development, i.e. limited investments and acquisitions.

Considering the high speed growth of the business ecosystems, the question arises how quickly the talent pool can catch up. On the one hand, these companies need large groups of employees; on the other hand, these companies need strong and visionary leadership. BATXL diverges significantly in their approach and openness to hiring external talents versus grooming their own talents. For instance, Alibaba fostered a lot of talents internally over the years and is open only to a limited extent to hiring-in people, such as Guan Mingsheng (2001) from GE, Deng Kangming from Microsoft (2004), and Wei Zhe from B&Q (2006); all domestic hires from foreign companies. Baidu is successful in attracting top scientist Andrew Ng from Google and other AI related talents from Facebook, AMD and top American universities. However, this is a recent phenomenon and focuses on the new business. In fact, according to observers and public impression, Baidu cultivated most of the high level leadership by themselves. Nevertheless, in January 2017 Lu Qi, VP of Microsoft Global, was hired as CEO of Baidu, which indicated a big step for Baidu's talent strategy. The other three companies are relatively open to hiring-in talents. For instance, Tencent's current president Liu Chiping, formerly of Goldman Sachs, was hired already in 2004 and Zhang Xiaolong, the inventor of WeChat, was also an external hire; by now half of the top management is externally recruited. Of course, Xiaomi is by nature very open, as their founding team consists of former successful entrepreneurs and business professionals from Google, Microsoft and Motorola. Later, they also employed former Google Android head Hugo Barra for their international expansion (he resigned early 2017). LeEco has a particular reputation for proactively attracting top level employees from competitors; for instance, LeMobile hired a lot of experienced engineers and professionals from Huawei, Lenovo and Meizu.

BAT has a similar approach and as we have seen in Chapters 2 and 7, BAT has developed into highly diversified business ecosystems. While their original strategic focus was clear and diverging, the business ecosystems have developed more organically (see Chapter 3 and Chapter 7 for their investment approaches) rather than a specific strategic plan. Therefore, we see that strategy making in these ecosystems have an emergent nature, playing into opportunities and mitigating all kinds of risks from market, technology and regulatory changes. However, Xiaomi and LeEco showcase a much more specific strategic focus, not only in rhetoric but also in actual business focus. Xiaomi is focused on developing cost effective digital driven smart hardware consumer electronics while LeEco is focused on developing smart entertainment and entertainment integration with hardware applications, platforms and content. The comparison of BATXL's growth is summarized in Table 9.2.

TABLE 9.2 Diverging business ecosystems of BATXL: growth

	Baidu	Alibaba	Tencent	Xiaomi	LeEco
Growth strategy	From complementary own product development to diversification by investment	From complementary own product development to diversification by investment	From complementary own product development to diversification by investment	From diversification by own development to diversification by investment and incubation	From related diversification to unrelated diversification, by own development
Hiring-in resources	Limited	Limited	Open	Born open	Proactive
Strategic focus?	No	No	No	Yes	Yes

9.3.3 Ecosystem mechanism

One core differentiating feature of these business ecosystems is the extent of interdependence between the different components of the business ecosystems. Connected to the origin and strategic focus of the five business ecosystems (and probably the entrepreneurial approaches of the founders), we see that the various components and businesses of BAT's business ecosystems appear to be strongly interdependent. This means that the core business of, for instance, Tencent's QQ and WeChat, is strongly dependent on the developments of their second layer, revenue generating applications of games, portal and complementary services. However, in the case of Xiaomi and LeEco, this is rather different. In the business ecosystem of Xiaomi, the outer layers, i.e. the various hardware products, are dependent on the OS MIUI, Mi fans base and to some extent the console, while the core of the OS MIUI together with Mi fans base can exist without the specific applications in the outer layer. For LeEco, we see again a different picture. The core of content production and platform is most of all a cash flow generating activity for not only the core but also, especially, the new initiatives. The core of the business ecosystem can surely be integrated in any type of display in those projects, but there's no specific dependence of, for instance, the LeSEE project's success on the content production and platforms. This is a crucial difference with the more tightly bound ecosystems of BAT and to a lesser extent also Xiaomi. We call this interdependence 'outside-in dependence'.

In general, looking at the mutual interdependence of different components, businesses and business actors in the ecosystems, which is not within the boundaries of one firm but a coordinated outcome within the business ecosystem, we see that the ecosystem has developed a competence to coordinate. Coordination refers to orchestration rather than giving directives. Based on the above analysis of the interdependence of the ecosystems, we conclude that BAT's business ecosystems have developed a coordination competence while LeEco appears less well coordinated and Xiaomi is somewhere in between.

Beyond the way the various components, businesses and participants interact in the business ecosystem, we also observe differences in revenue models. Looking at the revenue sources for the listed parts of the business ecosystems, we see that Tencent and LeEco have a more diversified source of revenue. While both have a dominant revenue source, such as income from online games (Tencent) and TV sales (LeEco), they have 50–60% of their revenues from at least two other sources such as transaction commissions, value added services and subscriptions. In contrast, Alibaba, Baidu and Xiaomi's revenue source is singular, ecommerce for Alibaba, advertisement income for Baidu and hardware sales for Xiaomi. From this it appears that Tencent and LeEco face less risks in terms of revenue sources. Nevertheless, for all five business ecosystems, the main source of income is still the core business. This suggests that the recent diversification initiatives have yet to become major revenue generators.

The business models of the five business ecosystems cannot be specifically described as business models refer to specific offerings, value propositions and customer segments. Considering the wide variety of offerings and customer segments, we will highlight key features of the business model approach for comparative purposes. Alibaba's business model is driven by synergy and complementarity to reduce transaction cost and increase efficiency while Baidu's business model is predominantly driven by transaction efficiency by reducing information asymmetry in markets. Tencent's business model is also driven by synergy, like Alibaba's, but is particularly strong in creating lock-ins with their customers and stakeholders, increasing switching cost for users. Tencent's business model is a classic case of creating a competitive advantage by creating network externalities; i.e. the more users adopt, the more value it creates. Then, Xiaomi's business model is typically characterized as an asset light business model with the following features: 1) fans marketing; 2) iterative software R&D and product design; 3) outsource components, production and delivery; 4) online sales. It is the particular business model, unusual in the consumer electronics business that allows Xiaomi to put quality products on the market for disruptively low prices. In contrast, LeEco's business model is based on heavy asset investment. Although the core of LeEco is their entertainment content and platform, which is mostly online, it would be misleading to say that this is 'light asset'. In particular, one feature of LeEco's content model is the acquisition and production of IP, which in many ways is also an heavy asset approach. Moreover, LeEco is investing heavily in production facilities for TVs, smartphones, cars and other hardware products. Table 9.3 summarizes the comparison of BATXL's ecosystem mechanism.

9.3.4 Innovation

The diverging business model approaches also have consequences for what kind of innovations these ecosystems develop and how they develop these innovations.

TABLE 9.3 Diverging business ecosystems of BATXL: ecosystem mechanism

	Baidu	*Alibaba*	*Tencent*	*Xiaomi*	*LeEco*
Inter-dependence in business ecosystem	Core and outer layers are mutually dependent	Core and outer layers are mutually dependent	Core and outer layers are mutually dependent	Outside-in dependence	Outside-in dependence
Coordination competence?	Yes	Yes	Yes	No	No
Revenue model (2015, listed part for BATL)	Search: 83%; Transaction services: 10%; iQiyi video: 7%	China retail: 75%; International wholesale: 7%; China wholesale: 5%; International retail: 2%; Cloud computing 2%; others: 9%	Game: 55%; SNS: 23%; Internet advertise-ment: 17%; Others: 5%	Mostly hardware sales	TV sales: 47% Membership and distri-bution: 29% Advertisement: 20%
Business model features	Driven by transaction efficiency by reducing information asymmetry in market	Driven by synergy and comple-mentarity to reduce transaction cost and increase efficiency	Driven by synergy to increase lock-in and switching cost for users, create network externalities	Asset light business model	Heavy asset business model: Expansion by developing and diversifying by their own product development and production

First of all, these five ecosystems are masters of combining different types of innovations. In these Chinese ecosystems, there's no exclusive focus on technology or product innovation. From the start, BATXL has cleverly combined different types of innovation and we refer to Chapters 5 and 7 for detailed descriptions. Nevertheless, we do find certain patterns of dominant types of innovation. For instance, Xiaomi is particularly good at business model innovation; as indicated before, a light asset business model is rather unique in the smartphone industry. Tencent has proven to be a strong product innovator with successful products QQ and WeChat and a whole range of new games. Alibaba's most successful product innovation is Alipay and Alibaba has subsequently developed an innovative ecosystem around Alipay with the full financial service integrator Ant Financial. Baidu's emphasis is much more on the technological core of their search products, for instance, the pio-neering technology of image search and deep learning. LeEco has developed an interesting business model for hardware sales: for instance, LeEco sells their TVs at a low price but always in combination with a subscription to their content services, thereby not only disrupting the hardware electronics price but also pulling in new users to their content services.

Since new product development is one of the dominant innovation approaches of BATXL, we compare their different approaches. Alibaba has proven to have a strong ecosystem for internally incubating new start-ups; see Chapter 4. The overall culture of knowledge sharing and opportunity seeking, in combination with certain institutionalized systems such as internal business plan competitions and resource available for intrapreneurs, facilitate the entrepreneurial climate in Alibaba's ecosystem. Baidu has a somewhat different approach that is characterized by quick prototyping and focus on technological advancements. For instance, at the very beginning Baidu as a start-up bested incumbent Google by quick prototyping on Chinese language search. Tencent's WeChat product has been developed by a specific multiple team parallel product development approach. An idle team proactively developed a disruptive innovation, WeChat, while the other teams developed more sustaining innovative products such as Q Message. Probably the most distinct new product development approach is that of Xiaomi: Internet Thinking approach and fans marketing with iterated, user centred high speed product development. The role of users and fans and quick upgrading of the product is the core of Xiaomi's product development. Moreover, Xiaomi not just invests in companies, but also incubates companies and, as of early 2017, have successfully incubated 30 products. Lastly, LeEco's approach to new product development is not clear but characterized by at least two features: each new project starts with hiring an external top scientist or professional in combination with a large availability of cash and strong media promotion.

In general, our Chinese cases indicate that ecosystems are not a hurdle or competitive threat, but when managed and understood well, can be a proactive tool to speed up innovation rather than delay innovation. It is not only about mitigating risks, it is about how a company proactively builds its own ecosystem and plays an orchestrator role. Table 9.4 summarizes the insights from the comparison of BATXL's innovation.

TABLE 9.4 Diverging business ecosystems of BATXL: innovation

	Baidu	Alibaba	Tencent	Xiaomi	LeEco
Dominant Innovation types	Product, technology and business model innovation	Product and business model innovation	Product and business model innovation	Business model innovation cost innovation	Business model innovation Cost innovation
New product development approach	Quick prototyping	Internal entrepreneurship incubation	Parallel development	Internet Thinking: fans marketing; iterated, product development; incubating new projects	Project based, hiring external talents, a large availability of cash

TABLE 9.5 Diverging business ecosystems of BATXL: incubation

	Baidu	Alibaba	Tencent	Xiaomi	LeEco
Incubation strategy	Baidu Entrepreneurship Centre	Baichuan Plan	Double Hundred Plan	One Hundred Xiaomi Strategy	None
Year of establishment	2013	2013	2015	2014	Not relevant
Number of incubation centres	Beijing, Chengdu, Suzhou, Xiamen, Tianjin	Suzhou, Hangzhou	20 locations	None by Feb. 2017 but announced	None
Number of new 'CEOs'	Hundreds	Hundreds	Hundreds	Limited	Limited
Start-up competitions	No	Yes	Yes	No	No

9.3.5 Incubation

Table 9.5 summarizes the incubation practices of BATXL. Incubation of new ventures has been an important part of BATX's innovation and expansion. In fact, BAT all have a specific plan that focuses on new venture incubation and combines direct support via funding and resource, with indirect support such as incubation plans, start-up competitions and entrepreneurship education. LeEco sees itself as one big incubator but according to observers and experts their innovative initiatives and new product developments fit better in the category of innovation and self-development new businesses, rather than incubation. As the table illustrates, these incubation initiatives are all recent and the results are not yet clear. Nevertheless, BAT has succeeded in incubating hundreds of new ventures. So much that popular business media speak of the 'Alibaba Club' or 'Tencent Club'. All in all, BATX are highly active in incubation activities.

9.4 Investment strategies of BATXL

BAT makes significant investments in terms of deals and investment amount while Xiaomi and LeEco were relatively conservative. In terms of total investment deals by the end 2016; as shown in Figure 9.1, Tencent was the only one that outnumbered Alibaba, Baidu was the least one among the old generation ecosystems and Xiaomi was much more actively compared with another newcomer LeEco.

As shown in Figure 9.2, it appears that BAT in general invested more companies since 2013 while Baidu was still relatively conservative with its pace. In 2016, BAT has all stopped the exponential growth and had fewer deals than the previous year. Xiaomi and LeEco both had their first investment in 2013 while their investment patterns afterwards were actually quite different. Xiaomi had a leap in 2014 and

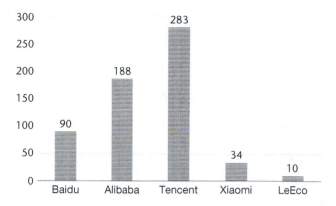

FIGURE 9.1 BATXL total investments comparison (end 2016; # of deals)

Source: author's own BATXL database.

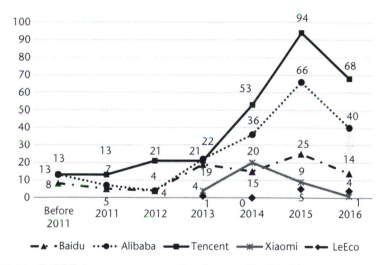

FIGURE 9.2 BATXL investments comparison by year (# of deals)

Source: author's own BATXL database.

then slowed down in 2015, which was probably related to the drawback of its core business. In 2015, although its smartphone sales volume still increased 15%, it was far below the market expectation; and in 2016, Xiaomi had a bigger challenge with a 36% sales volume decline, which certainly influenced its investment strategy. LeEco on the other hand has never followed a growth by investment approach. It became a bit more active since 2015 with a few deals. Nevertheless, a total of 10 investments in just two years is still considerable, especially when comparing to traditional industries and multinationals.

In terms of investment phase, as illustrated in Figure 9.3, it appears that the percentage of A round investments of BAT was similar (about 20%), while Xiaomi invested much more in the early phase ventures (38%) and LeEco seemed not so

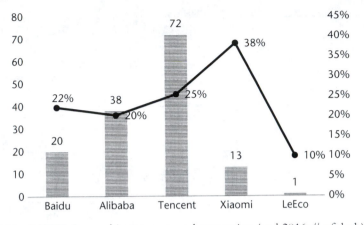

FIGURE 9.3 BATXL A round investments and proportion (end 2016; # of deals)

Source: author's own BATXL database.

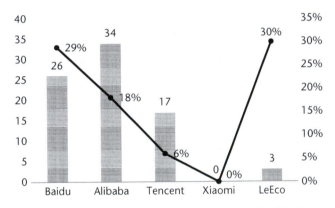

FIGURE 9.4 BATXL acquisitions and proportion (end 2016; # of deals)

Source: author's own BATXL database.

interested in early phase investment (10%). In terms of acquisition (see Figure 9.4), which normally means a late phase investment, we can see that Baidu and LeEco clearly paid more attention to acquisition (about 30%), while Tencent was more active with earlier phase investments than acquisition. Alibaba was somewhere in between and Xiaomi hasn't acquired any company by the end of 2016.

In terms of sectors, as Table 9.6 shows, the culture and entertainment sector has been one of the top two sectors invested by BAT by the end of 2016 (Baidu 15%, Alibaba 15%, Tencent 10%), which clearly indicates a strong interest from all the three ecosystems due to the large market opportunity. Besides the culture and entertainment sector, Alibaba had the most investments in the ecommerce sector (15%) which is the core business. Tencent's investments in the game sector was the heaviest (20%) which is Tencent's largest cash cow business so far. Following its 'connecting people to services' strategy, Baidu had the most investments in the LBS sector (13%). Moreover, Xiaomi and LeEco have quite different investment pattern

TABLE 9.6 Summary of BATXL's top five investment sectors

Ecosystem	Top 5 investment sectors
Baidu	LBS, culture and entertainment, ecommerce, education, enterprise services
Alibaba	Culture and entertainment, ecommerce, LBS, finance, enterprise services
Tencent	Game, culture and entertainment, ecommerce, healthcare, LBS
Xiaomi	Hardware is dominant, others include finance, culture and entertainment, healthcare, SNS
LeEco	Hardware and automotive

Source: author's own BATXL database

compared to BAT. Aiming to build a smart hardware ecosystem, half of Xiaomi's investments were in the hardware sector, which includes both consumer electronics like Bluetooth earphone and smart bracelet or household appliances like rice cooker and air purifier. While LeEco also showed strong interest in the hardware sector (about 30%), its ambition to build a next generation car was even more impressive; not only the number of deals but also the significant investment amount.

Summarizing, growth by investment appears to be a dominant approach for BATXL. In fact, the expansion by investment in a variety of sectors is remarkable in terms of number of deals but also in terms of variety of sector targeted. Moreover, even though BATXL all follows to some extent a growth by investment approach, we do observe significant differences in how to invest and what targets they invest in.

9.5 Competing or collaborating?

It is not surprising that the competition between the BATXL business ecosystems is significant, especially as they are offering digital driven online and offline products to predominantly consumers and online businesses. However, what is striking is that each of the ecosystems has started to compete in each other's original business field on top of diversifying in similar industries. Baidu is original in the search business but now Alibaba and Tencent are also investing several search services providers. Alibaba was and is still the king of ecommerce but Baidu and Tencent also set their feet in the field while Xiaomi and LeEco both developed the ecommerce platforms for their products. In particular, Tencent not only built a mini shop environment in the WeChat but also strategically invested in JD, the strongest competitor of Alibaba's ecommerce in China. Tencent originally is in social network services, in particular instant messaging, but all of the others have developed products in this field or invested in such companies. Xiaomi focused on consumer electronics and smart hardware, but by now all of them have entered smart hardware field, and LeEco is also competing in consumer electronics with SuperTVs and

TABLE 9.7 BATXL competing in the same emerging sectors

	Baidu	*Alibaba*	*Tencent*	*Xiaomi*	*LeEco*
LBS	Yes	Yes	Yes	Yes	No
Search	Yes	Yes	Yes	No	No
Ecommerce	Yes	Yes	Yes	No	Yes
Culture	Yes	Yes	Yes	Yes	Yes
Education	Yes	Yes	Yes	No	No
Enterprise services	Yes	Yes	Yes	No	No
Finance	Yes	Yes	Yes	Yes	Yes
Gaming	Yes	Yes	Yes	No	No
Healthcare	Yes	Yes	Yes	Yes	No
Hardware	Yes	Yes	Yes	Yes	Yes
SNS	Yes	Yes	Yes	Yes	Yes
Automotive	Yes	Yes	Yes	No	Yes

Source: author's own BATXL database

Le Superphones. LeEco's origin is in the entertainment field and especially given the good prospects for this sector, the others, in particular Tencent and Alibaba, have started to strategically invest and diversify into the culture and entertainment sector.

Besides the above direct competition in their original businesses, the five ecosystems have all expanded and diversified in a whole range of sectors. In Table 9.7 we combined the top five sectors for each of the five ecosystems, totalling 12 sectors (note: not 25 different sectors but a lot of overlapping sectors). We indicated which of the five ecosystems are active in which of the sectors. Active means either own products or invested in companies. The four sectors – culture, finance, hardware and SNS – are populated by all ecosystems. Moreover, BAT is operating in all the sectors. Therefore, the ecosystems are competing strongly in their own business fields and in the newly diversified sectors. It is important to note that the sectors are all emerging, high growth sectors, suggesting that there is enough market space for multiple players. Moreover, the extensive competition and lack of consolidation in combination with low entry barriers for new players, suggests that many of these sectors are still in the early phase of the industry life cycle.

The business ecosystems have not only competed for markets, but also have jointly created new ventures to disrupt traditional markets. One such example is Chinese taxi hailing platform Didi Chuxing. Not only the size of investments (over a billion USD) or market valuation (35 billion USD) is impressive. Didi Chuxing is claiming 10 million orders per day, 300 million users, 14 million drivers in over 400 Chinese cities. However, the current Didi Chuxing is an amalgamation of three companies. In 2013 young entrepreneur Chen Weixing founded Kuaidi Taxi in Hangzhou and Alibaba has been a significant supporter of Kuaidi from 2013–2015 with three rounds of investment. In the same year another young entrepreneur Chen Wei founded Didi Taxi in Beijing and Tencent has been a strong supporter of Didi from 2013–2014 with three rounds of investment. Then, in 2015 both companies merged into Didi Chuxing and both Alibaba and Tencent invested a combined two rounds of investments in the newly merged company. Moreover, Didi Chuxing invested 100 million USD in Lyft in September 2015, the main competitor of Uber in the US, which was also invested by both Tencent and Alibaba. The tie-up generates several avenues of cooperation, such as allowing users to summon rides through each other's network. Didi Chuxing is also expanding in Southeast Asia with investment in local taxi hailing companies like Ola and Grab. However, the taxi hailing business was still not safe from disruption as Didi Chuxing acquired Uber China in August 2016. In fact, this has pulled Baidu in the game, as Baidu had invested two rounds of investments in Uber China. Together, BAT (and other external investors such as Apple) has created within three years a super unicorn that has disrupted the Chinese taxi hailing market. It is just one example of how China's technology companies are not to be underestimated. Didi Chuxing is the only Chinese company with direct equity relationship with all three Internet giants Baidu, Alibaba and Tencent. The company has actually become a connecting point between the three business ecosystems.

Another interesting example is Meituan Dianping (also referred to as China Internet Plus or XinMeiDa in Chinese), a LBS platform with focus on catering and 15 billion USD market valuation. The current company originates in two companies. Meituan, established in 2010, received two rounds of investment from Alibaba. Dianping, China's earliest consumer review platform, established in 2003, was supported by Tencent with two rounds of investment. In 2015, both companies merged into Meituan Dianping. By 2016, 3.3 billion USD was invested by Tencent, DST and others. Here we see as well how Tencent and Alibaba have supported the rise of another super unicorn and by now Meituan Dianping is another connecting point between the business ecosystems of Tencent and Alibaba.

In fact, the above two examples are not outliers. For instance, Huayi Bro. Media Group, one of the largest public media companies in China, has received investments in 2015 from Alibaba, Tencent and Pingan. Interestingly, Ma Yun had already invested in Huayi Bro. in 2006 before the IPO. Both Alibaba and Tencent are expanding their culture and entertainment activities and this is one of their joint activities. Another example where the same three, i.e. Alibaba, Tencent and Pingan, invested jointly is Zhongan Insurance in 2013; see Section 5.3.4. It has become one of the most innovative online insurance companies in China. There are many more examples and from these we can conclude that the business ecosystems are not only competing but also collaborating.

9.6 Internationalization of BATXL

To what extent can business ecosystems be internationalized? While the internationalization of BATXL is still in the early phase and data and performance is relatively limited, in this chapter we will explore and compare Alibaba's internationalization with those of Baidu, Tencent, Xiaomi and LeEco. Alibaba's internationalization strategy has been extensively discussed in Chapter 6 and can be summarized as consisting of four components:

1. Cross border ecommerce: comprehensive and leading ecosystem consisting of Tmall International, AliExpress and Alibaba.com;
2. Overseas subsidiaries: setting up greenfield initiatives in the USA, Japan, Dubai, India and Benelux while absorbing a failed attempt in the USA;
3. Internationalization of services (Alibaba Cloud and Alipay): creating economies of scale for Chinese customers abroad, acquisition, establishing data centres and creating local partnerships;
4. Overseas investments and acquisitions: a diversified approach initially targeting the USA and nearby Southeast Asian markets with large scale investments and spotlight acquisitions.

With these strategic activities, Alibaba succeeded to a large extent in reaching its objectives, in terms of accessing new markets, upgrading domestic consumption, expanding current business, building reputation and successfully being listed in the USA. As indicators of success we see, for instance, Tmall Global's success in being the dominant platform for shopping for overseas products with close to 15,000 brands from over 60 countries. Alipay succeeded to become a major payment alternative for Chinese consumers abroad or domestic consumers shopping overseas. Alibaba now also boasts five subsidiaries and a newly launched global talent program to deepen the global presence and reputation. Lastly, Alibaba has invested in about 40 overseas entities in ten countries and 13 sectors, thereby significantly extending Alibaba's ecosystem footstep abroad and being close to overseas ecommerce and related technology developments. How did Baidu, Tencent, Xiaomi and LeEco fare in overseas waters? Table 9.8 summarizes our main insights.

Generally speaking, BAT's internationalization strategy also consists of both greenfield and expansion by investment approaches while Xiaomi and LeEco focus mostly on greenfield and do it yourself approaches with totally only one or two overseas investments.

In terms of the *greenfield* approach, Baidu was the one who started its internationalization the earliest by initiating Baidu Japan in 2006. Although the first attempt seems to have failed by its close down in 2015, Baidu never gave up its ambition of internationalization. Currently, Baidu has a clear focus on developing and promoting mobile software tools in overseas markets instead of its domestic core business search engine. The reason perhaps lies in the fact that it is almost impossible to outcompete Google in other countries. Nevertheless, Baidu's new

TABLE 9.8 Comparison of BATXL's internationalization strategies

	Baidu	Alibaba	Tencent	Xiaomi	LeEco
Business origin	Search	Ecommerce	Instant Message	Smartphone	Video
Year of establishment	2000	1999	1998	2010	2004
Foreign market entry	2006 Started Baidu Japan project	1999 Launched Alibaba. com	2005 Made an acquisition in South Korea	2013 Entered Taiwan, Hong Kong and Singapore	2016 Released Big Bang press in the USA
Number of offices	7 offices with about 1,000 employees	5 offices	N/A	N/A	2 offices with over 200 employees
International users or shipment (2016)	Baidu's mobile products have 300 million monthly active users by 2015	Tmall Global 14,500 foreign brands, 3,700 product categories, over 60 countries by 2016 AliExpress: 34 million sellers and about 100 million buyers, 243 countries covered by 2015	WeChat has 270 million monthly active overseas users by 2013	Xiaomi sold 6.5 million phones in India in 2016	N/A

(continued)

TABLE 9.8 Comparison of BATXL's internationalization strategies (*continued*)

	Baidu	*Alibaba*	*Tencent*	*Xiaomi*	*LeEco*
Revenues overseas	2015: 109 million USD, 1.1% of the total revenue	2015: 1.1 billion USD for international wholesale and retail, 9% of the total revenue	2015: 1.3 billion USD, 8% of the total revenue	2016: 1 billion USD in India, 10% of the total revenue	N/A
Overseas investments	15 deals	44 deals	79 deals	1 deal	2 deals
Focus countries and regions	USA, Southeast Asia, India, Egypt, Brazil	USA, India, Southeast Asia	USA, Southeast Asia, India	India, Southeast Asia	USA
Dominant strategy	Greenfield and acquisition	Import/export, greenfield, Investment and partnership	Investment	Partnerships	Limited relevance
Investment focus	Acquisition	Mixed	Early phase investment	Limited relevance	Limited relevance

Source: data compiled from authors' own BATXL databse, BATXL's company websites and annual reports

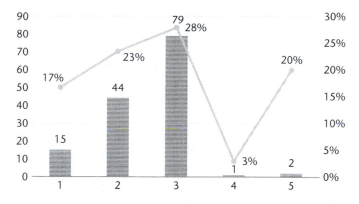

FIGURE 9.5 BATXL's total overseas investments (end 2016; # of deals)

Source: author's own BATXL database.

strategy seems to have worked well, given its significant improvement of the overseas performance in 2015. Tencent, on the other hand, not only continues its effort to internationalize the game business which is still in an early phase, but also put a high hope to its new core WeChat. Competing with other successfully instant messengers like WhatsApp and Line, it has achieved a certain user base in Southeast Asia, Europe and the US. Xiaomi started to sell its products to foreign countries in 2013, from Taiwan, Hong Kong to Singapore, India, Russia and Turkey. However, it never stops struggling with the internationalization, first the IP lawsuit by Ericsson in India, then the retreat from Brazil, and recently the leaving of its only foreign executive who was in charge of its internationalization strategy. The highlight of its internationalization was the 6.5 million phones sold in India in 2016. With a lot of unanswered questions, the only certain thing is that Xiaomi will still keep on going with its internationalization. LeEco has quite a different strategy compared to the other four ecosystems. On one hand, it was the one who started the internationalization the latest, i.e. in 2016. On the other hand, it was considered to be the most different one by direct entering the US market instead of first trying out in nearby region, i.e. Southeast Asia. Since it was very recent move, the overseas performance cannot be assessed now.

In terms of the *investment* approach, Tencent was the earliest overseas investor among the five ecosystems. Its first overseas deal went back to 2005, while Alibaba was in 2010 and Baidu in 2013, not to mention the other two newcomers. Tencent was also the most active one, with about 80 deals in total, in particular after 2013, along with its domestic investment boom. In contrast, Baidu was the least active one among BAT while Xiaomi had only one overseas investment (it invested Pebbles Interfaces, an motion detection technology start-up in Israel in 2013, which was acquired by Facebook in 2015) and LeEco had two (acquisition of an American TV producer VIZIO and an unclear investment of an American futuristic automotive company Faraday Future). Figure 9.5 compares the total number of overseas investment deals of BATXL and their relative importance. As Figure 9.5 illustrates,

Tencent is not only the largest overseas investor, their overseas investment deals also represent 28% of their total number of investments deals. It is also clear that BAT is following an overseas growth by investment approach while Xiaomi and LeEco are clearly not following this path. Generally speaking LeEco is not expanding by investment.

When we look at the number of overseas deals by year (see Figure 9.6), it becomes clear that overseas investment really started to take off since 2013. While on the one hand, the ecosystems strategically shifted focus to explore foreign markets, there has also been a strong competitive peer pressure, especially between BAT. Moreover, the successes and IPO of Alibaba has certainly fuelled this overseas investment and acquisition drive. Compared to the findings of Section 9.3, the growth of overseas investment is in line with the overall growth by investment approach adopted by the ecosystems since roughly 2013. LeEco's first overseas deal was in 2016, so it is too early to conclude anything on their performance, or approach for that matter. However, considering their domestic expansion approach by own organic but high speed development, it is not likely LeEco will change their approach anytime soon. Moreover, recent cash flow problems in fact have led LeEco to announce to slow down its foreign expansion. Overall, the number and timing of overseas investments suggests a strong strategic alignment with their domestic approach.

Then, the question arises, where do they invest in? Figure 9.7 summarizes our data on early phase investments by BAT, as LeEco and Xiaomi both have no early phase overseas investments. The patterns is quite clear: Tencent is strategically focusing on early phase investments, pre A or A round investments, accounting for over 40% of their overseas investments. Baidu and Alibaba have far less early phase investments, while Baidu is clearly not focusing on early stage ventures abroad and Alibaba is following a more hybrid strategy, with 16% in early phase, just like their domestic approach. From this we may conclude that Tencent is more interested in pioneering technologies and new gaming ventures overseas.

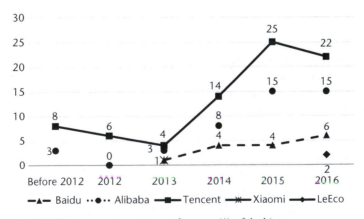

FIGURE 9.6 BATXL overseas investments by year (# of deals)

Source: author's own BATXL database.

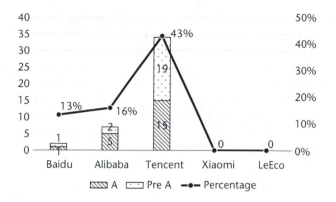

FIGURE 9.7 BATXL's A and pre A round overseas investments (end 2016; # of deals)

Source: author's own BATXL database.

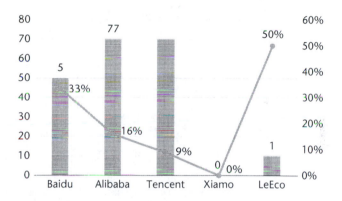

FIGURE 9.8 BATXL's overseas acquisition (end 2016; # of deals)

Source: author's own BATXL database

When we look at acquisitions, the other end of the investment spectrum, we see a completely different picture; see Figure 9.8. Baidu is standing out with 33% of their overseas investment being acquisitions, while Tencent only having 9% of their overseas investments in acquisitions. This supports the thesis that Tencent is mostly interested in early stage companies, while Baidu is mostly interested in mature acquisition targets. Again, Alibaba is following a hybrid model of investment, with 18% of investments in acquisitions. Generally speaking, Alibaba follows a rather balanced overseas investment approach with investments in all phases of ventures and companies. Tencent and Baidu have quite the opposite approach, the former one focusing more on early stage ventures, and the latter on acquisitions of more mature companies. It is noteworthy that LeEco's only two overseas investments, including one acquisition, and Xiaomi has no early phase investments or acquisitions abroad.

In terms of sectoral focus, we see a pattern that is similar to their domestic investments. Table 9.9 summarizes the top five investment sectors overseas by BATXL.

As we can see in Table 9.9, Baidu's investments have no specific sector focus while Alibaba and Tencent have preferred sectors such as ecommerce and the associated logistics for the former and games for the latter. Moreover, Tencent is an active overseas investor in SNS and digital healthcare. Xiaomi and LeEco invested in hardware related companies such as motion detection, TV and automotive. It is noteworthy that both Alibaba and Tencent have also invested in overseas hardware related companies. Another interesting patterns appears when we look in which countries these investments are, as summarized in Table 9.10. The target country for all except Xiaomi is the USA. Especially BAT is investing significantly in the USA, while LeEco's strategic focus abroad generally speaking is on the USA. BAT's strategic focus is not exclusively on the USA but on expanding in a more hybrid way with specific interest in Southeast Asia and India. Tencent is by far the champion of investment in the USA with over 50 investments in the last years.

Overall, the internationalization of BATXL has just started but all of the companies have made significant greenfield and investment efforts in expanding overseas. The above analysis suggests that the approaches vary and while BAT is strongly investment focused, XL is more organic, greenfield focused. Xiaomi has had severe

TABLE 9.9 Summary of BATXL's top five overseas investment target sectors

Ecosystem	Top 5 investment sectors (# of deals)
Baidu	Security (2), finance (2), enterprise services (2), ecommerce (2), culture and entertainment (2)
Alibaba	Ecommerce (10), culture and entertainment (5), finance (5), logistics (4), hardware (4)
Tencent	Game (29), SNS (10), healthcare (10), culture and entertainment (4), software tool (3), hardware (3)
Xiaomi	Motion detection (1)
LeEco	TV (1), automotive (1)

Source: authors' own BATXL database

TABLE 9.10 Summary of BATXL's top three overseas investment target countries

Ecosystem	Top 3 investment countries (# of deals)
Baidu	USA (7), Israel (2), other countries one each
Alibaba	USA (20), Hong Kong (6), India/Israel/Singapore (4)
Tencent	USA (52), South Korea (7), India (4)
Xiaomi	Israel (1)
LeEco	USA (2)

Source: authors' own BATXL database

setbacks in their internationalization but no intent to stop or slow down; the same holds for LeEco. Moreover, while Baidu is more interested in mature acquisitions, Tencent is focusing on early phase ventures. Alibaba is the most hybrid of all, with a variety of greenfield initiatives and extensions, such as Alipay and Alibaba Cloud, but also a mixed and balanced portfolio of overseas investments in a wide range of phases and sectors. Moreover, the ecosystems simultaneously follow a variety of approaches, best illustrated by Alibaba's four components of international strategy. We refer to 'hybrid models of internationalization' to include that variety of approaches.

However, the internationalization of BATXL has not gone smooth, as indicated earlier with the case of Xiaomi and LeEco. In particular, we see the following challenges that should not be underestimated (see Table 9.11). First, many of the Chinese business models are built around locally embedded ecosystems of companies, products and technologies; building up such locally embedded system will take at least as long as in China, and probably longer. Moreover, China has been a virgin land for such ecosystems, while markets like the US have mature competing ecosystems. Second, while the strong customer focus in China works well for Chinese tech companies because they understand the Chinese customers all too well, abroad this will not work so easily. Even equipped with big data tools, Chinese companies have little overseas market experience. Third, a lack of complementary services and infrastructure abroad such as connected banks, utilities, restaurants, taxis, to name a few in foreign developed markets, makes it more challenging to have the high speed development and growth of China. Fourth, as seen in the case of Xiaomi, the IP strategies of BATXL are probably not sufficient to deal with and engage in patent wars with overseas incumbents. Fifth, overall negative impression of Chinese

TABLE 9.11 Key challenges for internationalizing BATXL's business ecosystems

Challenges	Business ecosystem or context
• **Locally embedded and tied business ecosystems**	• Business ecosystem
• **Lack of overseas market experience**	• Business ecosystem
• **Lack of complementary services and infrastructure overseas**	• Context
• **Limitations of intellectual property management**	• Business ecosystem
• **Negative impression of Chinese products overseas**	• Context
• **Difference market positioning domestic versus overseas**	• Business ecosystem
• **Cash flow limitations and foreign investors**	• Business ecosystem

products abroad, despite the success of champions such as Haier and Huawei. Although this is a two-sided challenge, Chinese companies have a responsibility for their own sake to improve their foreign public image. Sixth, the market positioning of BATXL has challenges in overseas markets. Their domestic focus is often one of low price and medium quality, while this particular niche in China may be large, it may not be so large in overseas developed markets. Lastly, the abundance of capital available in domestic markets, supported by local investors and banks, may not be enough for foreign expansion at high speed. LeEco has clearly seen these limitations in the last year. Tencent is tying up with foreign investment funds to be more local but also to guarantee support from overseas investors. Alibaba has secured international investments early on, succeeded with a large foreign IPO, as had Baidu and Tencent, and have strong cash flows from their core ecommerce business.

Considering the above, we conclude that:

- the business ecosystems are internationalizing;
- the internationalization is of strategic importance;
- the business ecosystems follow hybrid models of internationalization;
- the internationalization of Chinese business ecosystems face challenges.

9.7 Insights from comparing BATXL's business ecosystems

Only by comparison can we draw lessons, therefore, in this chapter we have compared BATXL's business ecosystems. In particular we compared the founding, growth, mechanism, innovation, investment, competition and internationalization of BATXL. Our comparison draws on the Alibaba case of Part 2 and the discussion of the business ecosystems of Baidu, Tencent (Chapter 7) and Xiaomi and LeEco (Chapter 8). Moreover, in this chapter we have used our extensive BATXL global investment database to provide deeper insights into BATXL's internationalization. The following six insights about the BATXL business ecosystems stand out:

1. BATXL's business ecosystems are not the same but adopt diverging business models;
2. BATXL's business ecosystems are continuously transforming;
3. BATXL's business ecosystems expand by investing;
4. BATXL's business ecosystems have diverging investment approaches;
5. BATXL's business ecosystems are not only competing but are also collaborating on developing new ventures and expanding markets;
6. BATXL's business ecosystems adopt hybrid internationalization models.

We conclude that business ecosystems are not all the same and our case studies suggest that there are diverging models of business ecosystems. Moreover, business ecosystems appear to be continuously transforming and adapting and the features of the growth strategy, mechanisms and innovation support such flexible and transformative business approach. These insights also lead to questions. The comparative case study suggests that BATXL's business ecosystems are proactively transforming and do so in diverging ways and with different approaches thereby opening up new markets, technologies and niches. What are the specific advantages and disadvantages of this way of organizing business? Moreover, the five ecosystems have a proactive expansion approach, albeit in different ways. While Tencent is investing in hundreds of companies globally, LeEco is expanding by their own organic development with large sums of capital investments. Can Tencent absorb so many new ventures? Is LeEco expanding too quickly as suggested by their cash flow problems? Baidu appears to be most technology focused while Alibaba has a very balanced approach. Xiaomi has a specific approach with clear strategic focus where they basically invest in start-ups and adopt Xiaomi's business model. Which of these approaches works best, or in other words is most sustainable in the long run? Then, the findings suggest that business ecosystems are not only internally dynamic but are also showcasing fluid boundaries and are by no means exclusively competing but also collaborating amongst each other. Is this new way of organizing conducive to co-opetition and innovation beyond organizational boundaries? Lastly, the various internationalization approaches of BATXL have one thing in common, going global is a strategic must and the ecosystems spare no effort to make it happen. The initial performance appears to be positive and the outlook optimistic. Can business ecosystems be internationalized sustainably? In the final concluding chapter we will provide a discussion on the above and other contemplations.

10

CHINESE BUSINESS ECOSYSTEMS

Lessons from BATXL

10.1 Introduction

Alibaba, Baidu, Tencent, Xiaomi and LeEco have emerged as significant competitors in a variety of business sectors in China. They have not only lead but also created new markets, both in traditional and newly emerging sectors. Many incumbents and multinationals have been taken by surprise and newcomers have eagerly joined the game that BATXL has been orchestrating in the last decade. The success of BATXL can be largely contributed to their new organizational form, a business ecosystem, which has fostered the rapid growth and transformation of their businesses. In our concluding chapter we will discuss the insights and lessons of the Chinese business ecosystems based on a set of questions. These questions have been generated by our interaction with business leaders and experts asking 'What would you want to know about Chinese business ecosystems?'

1. What are business ecosystems?
2. How successful are the Chinese business ecosystems?
3. What are the competitive advantages of business ecosystems?
4. Which of the five Chinese business ecosystems is better?
5. What are the challenges of business ecosystems?
6. Do business ecosystems only function well in China?
7. Can business ecosystems be adopted in traditional industries?

10.2 What are business ecosystems? Five key features

We refer to business ecosystems as new organizational forms where the businesses are interdependent through a variety of equity relationships combining product and service offerings into a customer centric offering. While the boundaries of a business ecosystem are fluent and dynamic, we take equity relationships as a criteria to be part of the business ecosystem. We distinguish business ecosystems from companies, holdings and business networks. While acknowledging that no business ecosystem is the same, our case studies suggest that they share at least five distinguishing features. In what follows we will discuss each of the five features.

1. Digital enabled business

   The five ecosystems are enabled by digital technology. The digital enabled business allows for convenient communication and sharing of information across the ecosystem, rather than just between two actors. A business ecosystem facilitates the connections between a large groups of actors. BAT and LeEco are all born as digital companies, regardless of whether they started in ecommerce, instant messaging, Internet search or online video. Moreover, many of their businesses are dependent on the convenient and smooth connection between actors in the business ecosystem. While LeEco is now largely considered a hardware ecosystem, the digital 'glue' is ever present. Even Xiaomi, a hardware producer according to a traditional definition, also depends significantly on their own software operating system 'MIUI' and fans marketing, which focuses on making use of social media to bind customers. Digital technology has facilitated the way in which information is shared among the actors, products and services are co-created with customers and actors, resources such as capital and knowledge are exchanged and how complementarities between products, services and businesses are created.

2. Focal player as ecosystem orchestrator

   The five ecosystems all have one focal player as the gravity provider and network orchestrator in their respective ecosystems (cf. Boncheck and Coudary, 2013). For instance, Alibaba's core is comprised of four ecommerce platforms (Alibaba.com, 1688.com, Taobao.com, Tmall.com). The five focal players are in the centre of these ecosystems to provide initial resources, incentives, platforms, coordination mechanisms and reputation to attract and keep actors. If these focal players, the core platforms, step out of the ecosystem, there is no ecosystem left. It is notable that although the ecosystems of Xiaomi and LeEco also have focal players, their roles are not exactly the same as BAT. To some extent, the participants in these two ecosystems do not depend on the focal players as much as in the case of BAT. Nevertheless, in all five business ecosystems the focal player is a network orchestrator without the hierarchical authority of a company or holding (Dhanaraj and Parkhe, 2006). In contrast with other studies, our cases indicate that the focal player does not aspire to 'own' the customer in one specific domain (cf. Weill and Woerner, 2015). In contrast, the Chinese business ecosystems do not operate or focus on one specific domain but have a diversified business approach that centres on their core offering. Moreover, the ecosystems do not provide a one stop solution, single platform as for instance Amazon is offering. Also, they do not create a specific product lock-in, such as for instance PayPal, which can easily plug itself in all kinds of ecosystems. Our Chinese business ecosystems are the ones that adapt to the context, customer and competitor.

3. Interdependent set of business actors

    The actors in business ecosystems appear to be strongly interdependent (cf. Adner, 2006). The interdependence between the actors is not only financial and equity based, although a prerequisite to be part of the business ecosystem. The interdependence is found in growth strategies, investment approaches, and complementarities between offerings, business synergies and resource sharing. The ecosystems are by no means 'loosely coupled systems of autonomous firms' such as in innovation networks (Dhanaraj and Parkhe, 2006). Moreover, they are not plug-and-play Internet platforms such as Amazon or Apple where participants just perform business, largely independent of other businesses (Weill and Woerner, 2015). On the contrary, the Chinese cases show that business ecosystems have intricate and complex relationships of interdependence. For instance, Baidu's ecosystem core, search technology, and the second layer of the ecosystem, are mutually dependent; i.e. without the core the second layer cannot function optimally but also the other way around, without the outer layer, the core cannot provide a comprehensive offering. For Alibaba, the businesses in the outer layer of the ecosystem are strategically synergistic: value and business is created for one another. Economies of scale are created by the large user base of shoppers at the core of the ecosystem and the shared services such as online payment service Alipay, big data service Alibaba Cloud, smart logistics service Cainiao and communication service Aliwangwang. These are the 'glue' that keeps together the highly diversified business of Alibaba. The start-ups that Xiaomi invested in do not only copy Xiaomi's business model but also share the same fans base, design, brand and market reputation. Moreover their products are fulfilling different needs but of the same group of Xiaomi's fans. Therefore their equity based interdependence with Xiaomi has become also resource sharing and complementarity based, in particular due to the reputation effects. Although their mechanisms and specific operations may differ, the five business ecosystems share the high interdependencies between the business actors in the ecosystem.

4. Co-evolution with the business context

    The transformation of the five business ecosystem is not just a response to internal or external forces but a proactive transformation. These business ecosystems are first organically fitting themselves into the business context to meet the demands of the market, and then at a later stage proactively orchestrate the transformation of the business context by experimenting and exploring technology, product or business model innovations, and opening up new markets. Product differentiation by BATXL into Internet finance, digital healthcare and LBS such as taxi hailing are not externally forced; neither did the ecosystems face any financial or operational problems. Rather, the ecosystems followed emerging opportunities, from changing customer preferences, technological advances, and repression of certain monopolized sectors, while also adapting to regulatory and market changes. In particular in the case of the financial industry, it is clear that technology together with business are transforming the industry and its regulation. The strategic change is not forced by the business context, but the business ecosystem is co-evolving with its context. Understanding business ecosystems necessitates us to adopt a co-evolutionary perspective to show that the environment not necessarily determines ecosystem strategy and that ecosystem strategy is also not necessarily free of influence from the environment. In fact, both ecosystem strategy and environment co-evolve, in particular in an emerging economy where the environment is particularly dynamic and changing.

5. Cross industry diversification

Cross industry diversification is a key feature and the source of a competitive advantage of the five business ecosystems. The scope of the business activities within the five ecosystem is wide. BATXL has diversified the core business, such as Alibaba moving from B2B to C2C markets or internationalizing with cross border ecommerce, Xiaomi from smartphone to pad, and PC, and LeEco from film and TV video platform to moviemaking business and sports event platform. They have also diversified beyond the core and original industry. In particular, they have surprised many incumbents in traditional industries such as finance, healthcare, logistics and entertainment, by entering these industries with new and often disruptive service offerings. As in Adner's (2013) words, ecosystems provide the right 'lens' for spotting opportunities but, in contrast to his study, we observe that ecosystems are not passive integrated value chains that need to be mobilized. In fact, the ecosystem is a proactive, early warning system for new opportunities while at the same time providing a rich infrastructure of resources to act upon the opportunity: quickly prototype a new product, incubate a venture, invest in an emerging sector or acquire knowledge and market reputation and early internationalization into new geographic markets.

Four approaches to diversification and growth stand out: 1) investment; 2) incubation; 3) innovation; 4) internationalization. These approaches are not mutually exclusive and in many cases overlapping. Nevertheless, it illustrates the rich and rapid diversification approaches of growth. It is exactly the combination of a variety of approaches that allows these business ecosystems to be quick, relevant and competitive. Moreover, as we see in the Alibaba case, innovations and diversified offerings are not necessarily appropriated by the ecosystem or network (cf. Dhanaraj and Parkhe, 2006) but may lead to spin-outs and even exits out of the ecosystem. All in all, all the Chinese business ecosystems analyzed in this book are highly diversified businesses and grow by extensive entry into newly emerging sectors in China.

10.3 How successful are the Chinese business ecosystems?

In this section we will provide the available data and insights on the performance to give an indication of the comparative performance. We employ quantitative and qualitative indicators. Table 10.1 summarizes the main quantitative indicators for performance, based on availability and triangulated accuracy.

TABLE 10.1 The performance of BATXL

	Baidu	*Alibaba*	*Tencent*	*Xiaomi*	*LeEco*
Business origin	Search	Ecommerce	Instant Message	Smartphone	Video
Year of establishment	2000	1999	1998	2010	2004
Monthly active users (MAUs) or shipments in China	Mobile search: 660 million MAUs (Sep. 2016)	Mobile products: 493 million MAUs (Dec. 2016)	QQ mobile: 647 million MAUs; WeChat: 846 MAUs (Sep. 2016)	MIUI: 170 million registered users (Dec 2015); Smartphone sales volume: about 200 million (Dec. 2016)	LeTV: 86 million MAUs (Sep. 2016)
International users or shipment (2016)	Mobile product MAUs: 260 million	AliExpress: about 100 million consumers (2016)	WeChat: 100 million MAUs (2016)	Over 10 million smartphones sold in 2016	N/A
Employees	40,000	34,000	25,000	8,000	15,000
Revenues (2015, billion USD)	9.9	12.3	15.8	12	1.9
Revenue growth (2012–2015, compound annual growth rate)	44%	30%	33%	83%	121%
Net profits (2015, billion USD)	5.2	3.9	4.5	N/A	0.09
Net profitability (2012–2015, average)	39%	42%	28%	N/A	9%
Market cap (Jan. 2017, billion USD)	58	220	230	45	11

Source: data compiled from BATXL's company websites and annual reports, BigData-Research (2016), China Business Intelligence Net (2016).
Note: MAUs are in a given month, the number of unique mobile devices that were used to visit or access certain mobile applications at least once during that month.

Besides the above quantitative indicators, we have the following qualitative indicators of performance. Fast Company *World's Most Innovative Companies* 2017 Global top 50 list includes Alibaba (No. 11), Tencent (No. 12) and Xiaomi (No. 13), while Baidu is included in the China and AI/Machine learning global ranking. According to Forbes China (2015) publication '2015 China's mobile Internet top 30', Tencent, Baidu and Alibaba are the top three according to revenue ranking. The revenues of BAT combined are more than the remaining 27 companies on the list, suggesting the sheer size of these companies. Moreover, half of the remaining 27 companies in the list have already been invested by BAT, meaning they are already part of the respective ecosystems. Within the 64 Chinese unicorns in 2015, 50% are either spin-offs or have an equity investment relationship with BAT (Lieyun Net, 2016).

Except the smartphone sales and OS users, as indicated in Table 10.1, Xiaomi has succeeded in incubating 77 ventures, most of them early stage. Over 30 of these ventures have already launched their products in the market; the others are still in the R&D phase. Within the 30 ventures launched to the market, there are four unicorns and 16 ventures that have revenues over 10 million RMB and three of the 16 ventures have revenues over 1 billion RMB revenues. For instance, the Xiaomi smart bracelet is the number one market player in China and second globally according to sales revenues. Another example is the mobile electric charger, ranked number one globally with over 55 million chargers sold. Lei Jun claims that Xiaomi's ecosystem has now connected with 50 million smart devices, excluding smartphones. The overall revenue of the ecosystem is estimated to total 15 billion RMB, excluding the cell phone revenues, which was 12.5 billion USD in 2015 and not disclosed in 2016 (Sohu, 2016).

LeEco developed over a dozen new ventures, four of which have already become unicorns, according to Chinese Unicorn Ranking 2016 published by iResearch. For instance, LeMobile ranked number 15 in China with 5.5 billion USD market valuation and LeSports ranked number 18 in China. Moreover, Jia Yueting claimed that in 2016 LeEco's total revenue will surpass 50 billion RMB with almost 200% annual growth compared to 2015 (Sina, 2016).

All in all, all of the five business ecosystems have strong performance and high growth rates, in contrast to the many incumbents and newcomers in China and abroad. It should not be forgotten that China's market is highly competitive and full of unforgiving customers. Therefore, the current data suggests that the business ecosystem approach is not only one of rapid growth but also of high performance in the market.

If we would take a more stringent approach to assessing the sustainability of the performance of these ecosystems, we could adopt the common requirement of seven consequent years of above industry average performance as an indicator of sustainable superior performance. With this indicator, Baidu, Alibaba and Tencent all have a positive score and have achieved sustainable performance. For Xiaomi it is still too early to assess as the company has been established just seven years ago while LeEco's profitability is fluctuating and especially cash flow concerns require a more modest assessment of its sustainability. Therefore, based on our comprehensive performance assessment of the five business ecosystems, we can safely state that it is unlikely that BAT will fail anytime soon. In the words of Iansiti and Levien (2004), the ecosystems are sustainable due to their continuous productivity, i.e. new products, technologies, ventures, robustness (survival, and niche creation) allowing variety and wide diversification. Concluding, Chinese business ecosystems have succeeded to rapidly become high performers according to financial and strategic performance indicators.

10.4 What are the competitive advantages of business ecosystems?

We have already established in Section 10.3 that Baidu, Alibaba and Tencent have sustainable superior performances. What are the specific advantages that allow them to achieve above average industry performance? A competitive advantage allows an organization to outperform its competitors. Porter's classic approach is to distinguish cost advantages from differentiation advantages. However, such advantages only become sustainable if other organizations cannot easily implement, imitate or substitute for the same strategic approach. At the level of business ecosystems, which goes beyond single organizations but refers to a group of interdependent organizations with multiple strategic foci, the following question arises: What competitive advantage does a business ecosystem have to outcompete other business ecosystems, companies and organizations?

Our study of five Chinese business ecosystems and in particular the growth strategies of Alibaba provide indications of what makes these business ecosystems competitive. Our findings provide comparative insights from China for the established insights on the benefits of ecosystems in the USA by Adner (2006): platform leadership, keystone strategies, open innovation, value networks and hyperlinked organizations. While Adner (2013) suggests that ecosystems provide the right lens for spotting innovation opportunities, he treats ecosystems as integrated value chains and potentially a hurdle to effectively implement an innovation. However, our cases show that business ecosystems are a viable alternative strategy for innovation. The business ecosystems of BATXL are not vertically integrated value chains and to implement a new product or service, it is not necessary for all ecosystem participants to align or adopt the innovation. On the contrary, Chinese business ecosystems are a fertile ground for innovation, new ventures and disruptive business models. The advantages of Chinese business ecosystems can be summarized as follows:

- Facilitate innovation, especially *cross industry innovation* due to synergy, knowledge and resource sharing, digital enabler; allow larger industry variety and room for experimentation, therefore increase the chances of disruptive innovation
- Realize much *faster growth* than other organizational forms, in a proactive, strategic, as well as an emergent way, following emerging sector trends with the risk of failure

- *Shorter time to market* of new products and services with quick iteration after receiving feedback from the market, not only shortening the new product development and launch life cycle significantly but also being more relevant for the market
- Providing an excellent *incubation* environment: facilitate entrepreneurship and intrapreneurship due to decentralization, digital enabler, knowledge, and resource sharing
- The *strategic renewal capability* of business ecosystems allow them to not only adapt to changes in technology, market and regulation but also proactively be part of shaping the trends which makes them less fragile or more robust when facing contextual change
- The *coordination competence* of business ecosystem to orchestrate successfully across hundreds of business entities by allowing sufficient decentralized autonomy and power of decision making while at the same time connecting the local initiatives by shared users, business models and services such as cloud, payment and brand, makes it more difficult to be copied by competitors.

10.5 Which of the five Chinese business ecosystems is better?

In fact there is no such thing as a 'better' ecosystem; it is all about fit with the business environment. There is no optimal business ecosystem. The key advantages of business ecosystems include their capability to renew themselves and self-adjust. Therefore, it is not possible to just 'choose' one version, the core competence of a business ecosystem is a strategic renewal capability. This has far fetching consequences for business ecosystems.

For instance, Xiaomi's original business model is centred on an online light asset approach. However, since 2015 Xiaomi has noticed that there are also certain disadvantages of this approach; for instance, pure online sales channel became the bottleneck for its quick growth and resulted in Xiaomi missing the market opportunity in China's tier 3 and tier 4 cities where the consumers mostly buy smartphones offline. Moreover, Xiaomi's competitors have quickly caught up by learning Xiaomi's fans marketing approach as well as making advantages of their own strength, such as Oppo and Vivo's strong offline distribution network in China. While from 2010 to 2014 the online asset light approach worked well and gained Xiaomi a large market share in a legendary speed; by now this approach is no longer the best fit with the environment as well as the competition. Xiaomi has started to change by investing in more offline advertisement and flagship stores in 2016. In the annual meeting of Xiaomi in February 2017, an even clearer signal for change has been released by the founder, Lei Jun. He emphasized that ecommerce is no longer enough and the need for a new retail system which combines both online and offline resources. Obviously, although having experienced a significant sales drop in 2016, Xiaomi will not quit but keep renewing their business.

Another example is Tencent. While originally Tencent benchmarked and oftentimes copied games and software from other Chinese SMEs, the public war with its competitor Qihu360 in 2010, the second largest client software provider in China at that time, has strengthened its negative public reputation and finally led to a strategic adjustment of the company. Tencent changed the strategy from imitation to incubating ventures and building an open innovative ecosystem. The investments, both deals and amount, has risen significantly afterwards. Moreover, Tencent is not only fervently investing domestically but also overseas: they do not copy but buy part of or the whole company and/or related IP. Tencent has had their turning point in history and showcased a strategic renewal capability.

Of course, the strategic renewal capability and the specific approaches of the five business ecosystems are different, as we have seen in Chapter 9. Differences originate in the founders, ecosystem mechanism, and growth approach but also depend on the features of context, risk appetite and whether or not the sectors are newly emerging. All in all, the question would be, under what conditions does what business ecosystem approach fit best; emphasizing that 'what approach fits best' is changing and it is the strategic renewal capability that allows an ecosystem to fit best.

10.6 What are the challenges of business ecosystems?

Despite the advantages of business ecosystems, we cannot ignore the many challenges that business ecosystems face. In our discussion of Alibaba but also, for instance, Tencent and LeEco, we have seen that there are challenges related to the high speed growth and diversification strategy of business ecosystems. Here we summarize the key challenges of business ecosystems:

- Large debt and cash flow: While BAT has a lot of financial resources, it is no secret that BAT still needs to leverage large bank loans to finance its expansion. The extent of risk associated to the large debt is influenced by their cash inflow and stability of the revenue stream. Currently the revenues and profits of BAT are increasing, while at the same time the market potential is still existent. Moreover, as we have seen in the case of LeEco, the cash flow problems in 2016 have raised serious concerns about the sustainability of LeEco's non-listed businesses and it was a large capital injection by local investors that guaranteed the sustainability. Xiaomi also slowed down its investment pace when the main business, i.e. smartphone sales, experienced some setbacks in 2015 and 2016. How long can the business ecosystems keep up expanding by heavy investments?
- Management focus: The management teams of the BATXL ecosystems are overly focused on investments and expanding rather than ongoing business. An important consideration is that the sheer number and size of acquisitions and investments put significant pressure on their management. While most mature companies may settle for a handful of investments in one year, BAT and Xiaomi's business ecosystems, which are still young, are investing in dozens of projects per year and LeEco is expanding new initiatives rapidly. The question is how much time the management team needs to spend on this and

how many organizational resources, are needed for the various deals? Does the management of BATXL have enough time and energy left to focus on Alibaba's growth strategy and integrating all the new companies into the business ecosystem?

- Over-diversification: While diversification may lead to advantages of scope, synergy, risk reduction and market power, over-diversification may lead to more risk and more difficult synergy creation. BATXL all runs this risk once it is venturing in areas that they are not familiar with or have limited experience in. There is always a question which is difficult to answer: How much diversification is too much?

- Too large to orchestrate: The five business ecosystems are known for entrepreneurialism and spirit of innovation. However, for instance in the case of Alibaba with over 34,000 employees and a considerable portfolio of companies to run, Alibaba has but no choice left to increase management processes and bureaucracy. If the company grows so large so fast, will it become too large to operate? The challenges of orchestrating over one hundred business actors are not to be underestimated. Can Alibaba sustain its flexibility and agility that it is so famous for?

- New dominant player from within the ecosystem: While all the ecosystems have a strong and stable core, several new strategic nodes have become large businesses and mini-ecosystems themselves. For instance, Alibaba's Ant Financial node and LeEco's LeSEE node. Will these new nodes be willing to stay part of the business ecosystem? What if they become strong enough and are no longer to follow the original focal player? When will significant players leave the business ecosystem?

- Chinese roots: Is it possible to expand BATXL's business across national borders and gain significant market share abroad? Even though the Chinese Internet market is large, the EU and USA markets are equally interesting and full of potential. In particular, those markets are more sophisticated and demanding and may challenge the Chinese Internet business model. So far, the initial international successes are there, but the challenges of competing with established (American) ecosystems are large. The localized and highly embedded approach of the Chinese business ecosystems may not be so easy to implement outside of China.

- Limitations of corporate management systems and processes: Our research indicates that due to the high speed growth and limited business operation experience of BATXL, there are serious management challenges in coordinating resources effectively. As a consequence there are many redundancies and therefore waste of resources in these organizations. At the same time, that redundancy may also provide the necessary leeway for innovation, as we have seen with the idle product development team that eventually developed the disruptive WeChat service.

- Successor challenge: All of the business ecosystems are still first generation, founder led organizations. As in any large company found by an entrepreneur with strong charismatic leadership qualities, the challenges for the successor are significant. For instance, Ma Yun retired from his position as CEO in 2013 but he is still chairman of the board and doubtless the spiritual leader, Li Yanhong has no intention to retire but has recently put a heavyweight manager on the CEO position and Jia Yueting is obviously still very much the blood and veins of the company. All of them will face the successor challenge sooner or later.

10.7 Do business ecosystems only function well in China?

Clearly, there are business ecosystems outside of China. The common examples are from the USA: Google, Facebook, Apple, Amazon and Microsoft. Although the definition of business ecosystem varies widely, from supply chain to full blown stakeholder network, there is plenty of evidence that an approach where the organizational form is beyond the corporation is accepted. Nevertheless, the key insight is that business ecosystems can function well *regardless* of the contextual conditions, as long as the business ecosystem meets the five criteria as indicated in Section 10.2. A 'living' ecosystem will co-evolve with its environment. Therefore, the environment may influence the ecosystem but, on the contrary, the ecosystem also plays a role in shaping its environment. An ecosystem is an organizational form that grows and diversifies via transformation of the original core, complex investment and acquisition, internal entrepreneurship and incubation, continuous innovation and internationalizing the business. It is the combination of these growth approaches that make business ecosystems particularly relevant for newly emerging sectors and dynamic business contexts, such as China's. At the same time, there's no reason to believe that the same approach would not work well in more stable business contexts. Moreover, the business ecosystem approach allows greater flexibility, shorter time to market, quicker adoption of new technologies and an overall better responsiveness to customer, technology, competitor and regulatory changes. This surely is also a source of a competitive advantage in more developed markets as well. Therefore, business ecosystems are less fragile than traditional corporations and have the required agility to adapt to changing business contexts, regardless of where or when.

10.8 Can business ecosystems be adopted in traditional industries?

First of all, the five cases in this book span a spectrum of digital driven Internet companies but also include Xiaomi and LeEco's hardware ecosystems. In particular, Xiaomi's smartphone business initially and later other electronics and household appliances, and LeEco's smartphone and TV business and later automotive, are clearly invading traditional consumer electronics, appliances and automotive industries. Although the business approach and business model is quite different and potentially disruptive in those industries, it is clear that traditional industries can adopt business ecosystem approaches.

Second, traditional industries are not necessarily digitally disconnected. In fact, one may ask which part of traditional business operations could be digitalized or facilitated by digital technology. For instance, in the automotive industry many innovations are in the field of connectivity and Internet of things, while in the pharmaceutical industry, traditionally with long R&D processes, the innovations are coming from digital healthcare and ecommerce.

Third, is it possible that traditional industries change their role from directive leaders in their organization to becoming orchestrator of innovation initiatives inside and outside their corporate boundaries? Could many of these companies change their focus from dominating just one business domain and type of customer to diverse domains and customers? In fact, we have seen initiatives all around the world from MNCs like GE, Unilever, Michelin and Haier amongst others, to change the role of the corporation from director to orchestrator.

Fourth, there is no specific reason to believe why traditional businesses, including FMCGs, chemicals and manufacturers, could not develop a wider variety of business relations with other companies, ranging from investment, acquisition and partnerships to incubation of ventures. While the speed of such ecosystem development may not be as quick as BATXL's, the business logic would be similar. Especially, an emergent investment approach, often with multiple investment entities and external joint investments, would speed up and create larger flexibility.

Fifth, many companies are still responding passively to changes in the business context, while regulatory changes are in some cases only influenced by lobbying behaviour. Would it not be possible for companies to take a more proactive approach in shaping industries by adopting a business ecosystem approach? With many more 'tentacles' and vested interests in a large variety of complementary businesses, the companies would not only be better up to date, but also closer to influencing the direction, by orchestrating rather than directing.

Lastly, while many MNCs have diversified businesses, the approach is one of strategic road maps rather than a focus on following emerging sectors and technologies. This means that MNCs need to change the habit from minimizing risk to accepting failure and quickly moving on to the next opportunity. Speed of diversification is often more important, at least in China, than the precise prediction of the conditions of the opportunity. All in all, we believe that the business ecosystem approach as followed by the five Chinese cases in this book may provide fruit for thought for companies in newly emerging and traditional industries.

10.9 Concluding remarks from the authors: What can we learn from BATXL?

The insights from the BATXL cases are numerous and as authors of this book we strongly recommend other companies, both large and small, international and local, in traditional or newly emerging industries, to take up relevant lessons and inspiration. Whether it is lessons related to their continuous innovation and significant incubation practices, or growth by diversification and strategic investment, the business ecosystems of BATXL at least provide food for thought on strategy, innovation and business growth. However, the most significant insight for the authors is that the business ecosystems of BATXL are combining so many initiatives, approaches and practices simultaneously with the sheer purpose of growth and innovation, as a source of their competitive advantage.

10.10 Recommendations for future study

We hope that this book has not only provided a deeper look into Alibaba's business ecosystem and a detailed analytical comparison with four other Chinese business ecosystems, but also provides researchers with inspiration to further study business ecosystems in a comparative context. We believe that comparing Chinese business ecosystems with business ecosystems from developed markets such as the US and Western Europe, but also emerging markets like India and Brazil, will be highly insightful. Moreover, we believe that our study has opened up new avenues for research in the field of strategic management. In particular, we have analyzed the growth strategy of an ecosystem in much detail and also observed specific competitive advantages of a business ecosystem. Our study warrants further investigation, both inductive research in different country contexts but also deductive testing of some of the insights that were formed in this book with other cases or surveys. Lastly, with this book we also aim to provide a thick description of a new organizational form in a new business context and believe that we have illustrated the power of such an approach. Further studies should consider using detailed comparative case studies on business ecosystems to develop a deeper understanding of the dynamics and diversity of this business approach.

References

Adner, R., 2006. 'Match your innovation strategy to your innovation ecosystem', *Harvard Business Review*, 84 (4), pp. 98–107.

Adner, R., 2013, *The wide lens: What successful innovators see that others miss*, New York, Portfolio/Penguin.

BigData-Research, 2016. 2016 Nian di 3 ji du zhong guo zai xian shi pin shi chang yan jiu bao gao [2016 Q3 China online video market research report]. Available at: http://www .bigdata-research.cn/content/201611/368.html. Accessed 30/12/2016 [in Chinese].

Boncheck, M. and Coudary, S.P., 2013, 'Three elements of a successful platform strategy', *Harvard Business Review*, Available at: https://hbr.org/2013/01/three-elements-of-a-successful-platform. Accessed 24/09/2016 [online version].

China Business Intelligence Net, 2016. Xiao mi gong bu MIUI yong hu shu liang yi jing lei ji 1.7 yi lian wang ji huo [Xiaomi announced that the number of MIUI users has accumulated 170 million online activations]. Available at: http://www.askci.com/news/ chanye/2016/01/15/134832ygtl.shtml. Accessed 30/12/2016 [in Chinese].

Dhanaraj, C.Parkhe, A., 2006. 'Orchestrating innovation networks', *Academy of Management Review*, 31 (3), pp. 659–669.

Fast Company, 2017. The most innovative companies of 2017. Available at: https://www.fastcompany.com/most-innovative-companies/2017. Accessed 20/02/2017.

Forbes China, 2015. 2015 Zhong guo yi dong hu lian wang 30 qiang [2015 China's mobile Internet top 30]. Available at: http://www.forbeschina.com/event/188. Accessed 30/12/2016 [in Chinese].

Iansiti, M. and Levien, R., 2004. 'Strategy as ecology', *Harvard Business Review*, 82 (3), pp. 68–78.

iResearch, 2016. 2016 Zhong guo du jiao shou qi ye gu zhi pai hang bang Top 300 [The 2016 Chinese unicorn valuation ranking top 300]. Available at: http://www.askci.com/news/hlw/20160701/08481236430.shtml. Accessed 30/12/2016 [in Chinese].

LieyunNet, 2016. IT ju zi wen fei xiang: chuang qi zhi you 1% zou dao shang shi, du jiao shou yi ban yi shang you BAT xue tong [IT Juzi Wen Feixiang: only 1% of start-ups can be listed, half of unicorns have BAT blood relationship]. Available at: http://www.lieyunwang.com/archives/159641. Accessed 30/12/2016 [in Chinese].

Sina, 2016. Le shi: ji ji jie jue zi jin wen ti, 2016 nian le shi sheng tai shou ru jiang chao 500 yi [LeEco: solve the capital problem actively, LeEco ecosystem will reach over 50 billion RMB revenue in 2016]. Available at: http://finance.sina.com.cn/stock/s/2016-11-09/doc-ifxxneua4539378.shtml. Accessed 30/12/2016 [in Chinese].

Sohu, 2016. Lei Jun: Xiao mi sheng tai lian qi ye yi 77 jia [Lei Jun: there are 77 Xiaomi Eco-chain companies]. Available at: http://it.sohu.com/20161220/n476408696.shtml. Accessed 30/12/2016 [in Chinese].

Weill, P. and Woerner, S.L., 2015, 'Thriving in an increasingly digital ecosystem', *MIT Sloan Management Review*, 56 (4), pp. 27–34.

Index